Sāman Chants :

(In Theory and Present Practice)

Rāga Nṛtya Series No. 9

Sāman Chants :

In Theory and Present Practice

(with a Cassette of Sāman Chants)

G.H. TARLEKAR

Sri Satguru Publications
A Division of
Indian Books Centre
Delhi - 110007

Published by:
Sri Satguru Publications
Indological and Oriental Publishers
A Division of
Indian Books Centre
40/5, Shakti Nagar,
Delhi-110007
(INDIA)

First Edition: Delhi, 1995

ISBN 81-7030-440-7

Printed at : Mehra Offset Press, New Delhi.

Printed in India

Preface

After studying the relevant *Sāman*-literature and the recordings of the *Sāman* chants sung by expert chanters of the various traditions available at present, I thought it proper to place before the readers the theory and the present practice of *Sāman* chanting. I presented my first work in regard to this study - The *Sāman* Chants - A Review of Research. It was published by Indian Musicological Society, Baroda, in 1985. In this book, I have given the views of Western and Oriental scholars in regard to *Sāman* chanting and added my comments in each case. Now, in this book, I have attempted to state the theoretical approach to this subject as found in the relevant Sāmavedic works and the present state of *Sāman* chanting. I travelled through the various parts of the South and North India and recorded the chantings of some *Sāmans* indicative of the significant manner of each school. The chanting of the three schools of Sāmaveda is available at present - namely, Kauthuma, Rāṇāyanīya and Jaiminīya. The Kauthuma school exists in the South and the North (mainly, Gujarat). The followers of Rāṇāyanīya school are found in Karwar (Karnataka) and Andhra. The Jaiminīyas belong to two traditions namely, Tamilnadu and Nambudiri.

I shall always remain in debt to the various Pandits who allowed me to record their chanting of *Sāmans*. I must thank sincerely late Dr. V. Raghavan and Pandit Tatacharya Agnihotri who helped me by introducing the expert chanters in regard to the recording of the *Sāman* Chants. Dr. E.S. Srikrishna Sarma deserves my thanks, who allowed me to record some *Sāmans* from his tapes. Pandit Jogalekar of Gokarna helped to contact the expert Pandits of Rāṇāyanīya tradition in Karwar. My thanks are due to these respectable friends. I must thank Dr. C.G. Kashikar and Dr. R.N. Dandekar who have encouraged me always in my efforts in regard to my Sāmavedic studies. I particularly owe my debt to Dr. B.R. Sharma whose Introductions to the P.S. proved valuable. I am also indebted to Prof. (Miss) Shashikala Shirgopikar and Dr. Sudha Patwardhan for helping me in the rendering of the Hindustani notations of the *Sāman* Chants, included in this book. I cannot express in words the valuable help rendered by my wife in the writing and preparing the press-copy of this book. I should not forget to thank my friend Dr. Wayne Howard whose Sāmavedic studies have given me great help. Shri L.S. Rajagopalan of Trichur was always ready to help me. My sincere thanks are due to him.

I must thank Shri Naresh Gupta, Director, Indian Books Centre for readily accepting this book for publication.

PUNE

G.H. TARLEKAR

Contents

Abbreviations

A.G.	—	Āraṇyagāna
Ūha Daśa	—	Ūha Daśarātraparvan
Ūha Eka	—	Ūha Ekāhaparvan
Ūha Prā	—	Ūha Prāyaścittaparvan
Ūha Sam	—	Ūha Saṁvatsaraparvan
Ūha Kṣu	—	Ūha Kṣudraparvan
U. Ar.	—	Uttarārcika
G.G.G.	—	Grāmegeyagāna
Nār. S.	—	Nāradīyaśikṣā
Pūr	—	Pūrvārcika
P.S.	—	Puṣpasūtra
R.G.	—	Rahasyagāna or Ūhyagāna
Ṛv.	—	Ṛgveda
S V.	—	Sāmaveda
S.V. Br.	—	Sāmavidhānabrāhmana
1 Taiprā	—	Taittirīyaprātiśākhya

Sāman Chants
(In Theory and Present Practice)

PART I - THE THEORY

(a) Introduction

The word *sāma* is explained in the Vedic literature as consisting of two words namely *sā* and *ama*. Atharvaveda[1] (14.2.71) states - 'I am *ama* and thou art *sā* (i.e. ṛc). Sāyaṇa explains - '*sā* indicates *ṛc*, *ama* indicates the *svara* connected with it, which is of the nature of the expanse of the musical notes *ṣaḍja*, *ṛṣabha* etc. The Aitareyabrāhmaṇa[2] (12.12) says that the appellation *sā* stood for the *ṛc* and *ama* for the *sāma*. According to the Bṛhadāraṇyakopaniṣad[3] (1.3.22) *sā* and *ama* (together) bring out the *Sāman*-nature of the *Sāman*. The Chāndogyopaniṣad[4] (1.6.7) states that the *Sāman* is based on the *ṛc*. The Sāmavidhānabrāhmaṇa[5] (p.13 ed. by Dr. Sharma) explains that the word *sāma* is derived from *samatā* (equality). When the *Sāman*-singer chants the *Sāman* based on the Gāyatrī-metre, in the Bṛhatī-metre, the one based on the

Bṛhatī-metre, in the Jagatī-metre and that based on the Jagatī-metre, in the Triṣṭubh-metre it attains equality or commonness. The *Sāman* chanted in these different metres maintains sameness.[6] In the Jaiminīyabrāhmaṇa (p. 570 ed. by Dr. Raghuvira), the derivation of the word *sāma* is given from the word *sameta* (i.e. combined; *sam* + i = means to combine) [The *ṛc* and the *yajus* are combined in it]. In the Nirukta[7] (7.12.4), the explanation given is as follows:

(1) The *Sāman* is commensurate with the *ṛc* (*ṛcā sammitam*);

(2) It is the last in the order of performances (from *'so'* meaning to bring to an end or complete);

(3) It is cast or superimposed on the *ṛc* (from 'as' meaning to throw); it is equal to the *ṛc* (*ṛcā samam*). Jaimini (II.1.36) says that the *sāma* is the appellation for *gītīs*, (*gītiṣu sāmākhyā*).

The *Sāman* is to be understood as the musical rendering of the *ṛc*. The word *Sāman* occurs in the Ṛgveda in the sense of a chant sung (by the *Udgātṛ*), (e.g. Ṛgveda - I.173.1; II.43.2; VIII.95.7; VIII.98.1 etc.). The word sāmanya (Ṛgveda - IX.96.22) denotes the chanter, who is expert in the

Sāman-music. The particular *Sāman*-names like Rathantara, Bṛhat, Vairūpa, Śākvara, Raivata etc. appear in the Vedic Saṁhitās. The name Rathantara is explained by Sāyaṇa as the *Sāman* which becomes the means of the speed of the chariot (of the god); (*ratha* + *tṛ* + *a* - see Pāṇini - 3.2.46 and 6.3.67)

The *Gāyatrins* mentioned in the Ṛgveda (I.10.1) are explained by Sāyaṇa as the *Udgātṛs* who chant Gāyatra-sāmans. The *gāthins* occurring in this *ṛc* are the *Udgātṛs*, who chant *gāthās*. The *Yamagāthās* are referred to in the *Taittirīya Saṁhitā* (5.1.8), which are the *ṛcs* containing the praise of Yama. The references found in the Ṛgveda regarding the chanting of *Sāmans*, give the idea clearly that the distinction between the recitation of the *ṛcs* and singing of *Sāmans* was well-known in the period of the Ṛgveda. It is possible to understand that in the very early stage, the duty of the *Udgātṛ* was not so specialised. In the course of time, special musical knowledge became a necessity for the priest who chanted *Sāmans* in contrast to the Ṛgvedic priests who recited *ṛcs* at the performance of sacrifices. Thus the functions of the *hotṛ* (who recites *ṛcs*) and the *Udgātṛ* became distinguished from each other. The *Sāmaveda Saṁhitā* was thus connected with the *Sāmagas* (the *Sāman*-chanters).

(b) The Saṁhitā of Sāmaveda

The Sāmaveda Saṁhitā is divided into two parts - (1) *Ārcika* or *Chanda-ārcika* and (2) Gāna. Ārcika is again divided in to two parts - (i) Pūrvārcika and (ii) Uttarārcika. The former contains in the five chapters of the three *kāṇḍas*, Āgneya, Aindra and Pāvamāna, *ṛcs* numbering 585 given individually that are the basis of individual *Sāmans*. In the sixth chapter, called *Āraṇyakakāṇḍa* there are 55 *ṛcs*. There is the Mahānāmnī-ārcika in the end which is a *pariśiṣṭa* containing 9 *ṛcs* (10 according to the edition by Pandit Viṣṇudeva-ācārya). In the *Uttarārcika*, the *ṛcs*, the basis of *Sāmans* sung in the sacrifices in a fixed order are given in the form of *sūktas* (the groups of *ṛcs*), a large majority having 3 *ṛcs* each. There are about 400 *sūktas* in the *Uttarārcika*. There are some *sūktas* having more than 3 *ṛcs*. The total number of *ṛcs* in the *Uttarārcika* is 1225. Certain melodies are restricted to certain *ṛcs*.

The normal rule of the *Sāman*-singer is that the *stotra* is fashioned out of a *sūkta*. The *Sāman* employed in the first *ṛc* is chanted in the two other *ṛcs* of the *tṛca* (the group of 3 *ṛcs*) forming the *stotrīyās*. Stotras are formed from the chants of the *Uttarārcika*. The *stotras* are groups of varying number of stanzas from 1 to 12 each. In the Pūrvārcika the arrangement of the stanzas is determined by the consideration of metre and deity while in the *Uttarārcika* by the order of principal sacrifices. The *Udgātṛ* and his assistants learn the melodies first from the *Pūrvārcika* and then the *stotras* from the *Uttarārcika*.

When the *Sāman* is sung in one *ṛc* in a *stotra* it is called *ekarcagāna*. In the *pragātha* there are two *ṛcs* which are arranged into three and then sung. The total number of *ṛcs* in the *Pūrvārcika* and the *Uttarārcika* together comes to 1875. The majority of the *ṛcs* is from the Ṛgveda. There are 61 repetitions in the case of the *ṛcs*.

The *gāna* texts are four: (1) Grāmegeyagāna; (2) Āraṇyakagāna or Araṇyegeyagāna; (3) Ūhagāna and (4) Ūhya or Rahasyagāna. The first two comprise the Prakṛtigāna or Pūrvagāna. Grāmegeyagāna is also called as Veyagāna. The first two *gāṇa* texts are attached to the *Pūrvārcika* and the last two to the *Uttarārcika*.

Grāmegeyagāna has the melodies that were to be chanted in the village. The Āraṇyakagāna consists of those melodies which were to be studied in the forest as these were thought as dangerous in character. The Ūhagāna has the *Sāmans* which are to be used for the *stotras* that were to be employed in sacrifices. The *Sāman* of the *yoni* (the basic *ṛc*) is to be employed in the case of the other two *ṛcs* of the *tṛca*. The *tṛcagāna* is to be employed at the time of the sacrifice after guessing from the Yoni text. Hence the name Ūha is given for this *gāna*-text significantly. The former Vedic teachers have guarded the *gānas* for sacrificial use in the form of the *stotras* after having guess work and included them in the text of *Ūha*. Hence the *Mīmāṁsakas* called it as of human authorship (*pauruṣeya*). Ūhya or Rahasyagāna is based on the Āraṇyakagāna. Ūha and Ūhya are attached to the *Uttarārcika*.

(c) The Vedic Accent

The *ṚV* has three accents. This accent is called as *svara*. The word is derived from the root '*svṛ*' meaning 'to sound.' The three accents are *udātta*, *anudātta* and *svarita*. The *udātta* is unmarked; *anudātta* is shown by a horizontal line below the syllable while *svarita* is indicated by a vertical line over the syllable. The *svarita* given in the Prātiśakhyas as eight-fold, is divided in two main divisions as dependent (*sāmānya* or *āśrita*) and independent (*viśeṣa* or *anāśrita*). The *anudātta* coming after the *udātta* is turned into *svarita*. This is called the dependent *svarita* as its position depends on that of the *udātta*; e.g. - *sa̱hasráśīrṣā̱ purúṣaḥ sahasṟā̱kṣaḥ sa̱hasrápāt.*

The *anudāttas* coming after the *svarita* are called *pracaya* and are left unmarked like the *udātta*. Pracaya is also called *udāttaśruti* or *ekaśruti*. If the *anudātta* coming after the *udātta* is followed by the *udātta* or *svarita*, it is not turned into *svarita* but remains as *anudātta* only. That is why the last syllable in the group of *anudāttas* following the *svarita* is changed into *anudātta* when followed by *udātta* or *svarita*. In the above illustration the vowel *a* of *ha* in the word *sa̱hasráśīrṣā* has *udāttasvara* and the vowel *a* in *ra* has *anudāttasvara*; hence the *a* in *ra* is changed into *svarita*. The vowel *ī* in *śī* and *ā* in *ṣā* are both *anudāttas* which should have *udātta-śruti*; but the vowel *ā* in *ṣā* is followed by the vowel *u* in the syllable *pu* which is *udātta*. Hence it is marked with horizontal line below it indicating its position of being the *anudātta*.

The etymological meaning of *udātta* is *uccaiḥ ādīyate uccāryate* (*ut* + *ātta*). Technically the vowel of the syllable which is uttered taking resort to the upper portion of the throat, palate etc. is called as *udātta*. The *udātta* perceived as a high pitch is rendered by the word 'acute.' There is generally one *udāttasvara* in every word, leaving aside the exceptions; the remaining syllables of the words have *anudāttasvara*. In the words denoting the names of deities in a *dvandva* compound, there are two or even more than two *udāttas* e.g. *Indrābṛhaspatí*. The infinitive in *tavai* has for both the first and the last syllable, *udātta* accent. The *anudātta* is the grave or low pitch. Technically it is the accent of the vowel which is uttered resorting to the lower part of the throat, palate etc. Svarita is technically explained as the *samāhāra* of the *udātta* and the *anudātta*. Samāhāra means combination.

Svarita is rendered by the term circumflex. The dependent *svarita* has four varieties:

(1) *Tairovyañjana* - In this variety the intervening consonant is there e.g. '*agni*[1]*mīḷe*.' Here between the *udātta* vowel '*i*' of *gni* and the *anudātta* '*ī*' the first syllable of *īle*, the consonant '*m*' intervenes, still the *svarita* is resulted.

(2) *Vaivṛtta* - *Vivṛtti* means the absence of *sandhi* between two vowels where *sandhi* should have taken place - e.g. satyā-*nṛte* ava.... There is no *sandhi* of the *udātta* vowel '*e*' in '*te*' and the *anudātta* '*a*' in 'ava' still the vowel *a* is turned into *svarita*.

(3) *Tairovirāma* - In the *padapāṭha* of compounds, there is the short intervention of the time unit of a *mātrā*. Even with this intervention, the *svarita* results, e.g. '...goऽpátau.' In this illustration, the short time-unit of *mātrā* intervenes between the *udātta* vowel '*o*' of '*go*' and the *anudātta* vowel '*a*' of '*pa.*' Still the vowel '*a*' has the *svarita* accent.

(4) *Tāthābhāvya* - In this variety the *anudatta* in the midst of two *udāttas* is changed to *svarita* e.g. *tanūnapāt*. Here the *anudātta* vowel *ū* is placed in the midst of the *udātta* vowel *a* of the syllable *ta* and the *udātta* vowel *a* of the syllable *na*.

(5) *Prātihita* - When in two separate words, the first word has the last syllable accented as *udātta* and the second word has the first syllable accented as *anudātta*, and this *anudātta* is changed into *svarita*, it is called *prātihita*;

'*iṣe* | *ttvā* | *ūrje* | *ttvā*| = *iṣetvo*-rjjetvā.' Here the *anudātta* vowel *ā* of the second word *tvā* is changed into *svarita*.

The independent *svarita* has four varieties:

(1) *Jātya* - The *svarita* which is in the word originally, is called *jātya*; e.g. क्वं, कन्यां etc. It appears that such type of *svarita* is found in the word if it has a *yaṇ sandhi*. [In the *yaṇ sandhi*, the semi-vowels y, v, r, l are the substitutes of the corresponding vowels i, u, ṛ and ḷ (long or short) when followed by a dissimilar vowel.] In this type the vowel preceding the *svarita* may or may not be *anudātta*.

(2) *Abhinihita* - In this variety, the ending vowel *e* or *o* of a word is followed by *a* which is merged with them e.g. te | *avardhanta* = *teśvardhanta*.

(3) *Kṣaipra* - In this variety the vowels i, u, ṛ, ḷ when followed by dissimilar vowels, are changed into y, v, r and l respectively. e.g. *abhi* | abhi = *abhyabhi*, vi | undanti = vyundanti.

(4) Práśliṣṭa - In this variety, such cases of *sandhi* occur when a simple vowel followed by a homogenous vowel, the substitute for both is the corresponding long vowel; e.g. *ā* | adhattam = ā́dhattam; *sruci* | iva = *srucíva*.

(d) Accentuation of the Sāmaveda

In the *ārcika*, *udātta* is marked by numeral 1 over the syllable, *svarita* by 2 and *anudātta* by 3 e.g. *ṚV* (VI.16.10) -
1 3 1 2
v̲ītaye → SV (G.G.G.1) *vītaye*. When there are more than one *udāttas* successively, the first is only marked; e.g. (*ṚV*
31
VIII.71.1) - *pāhi viśvásyā̲ arā́teḥ* | (*SV. Pur* 1.1.6) - *pāhī*
2 3 1 2
viśvasyā arāteḥ|

Hi and *vi* are both *udāttas* occurring successively. The first *udātta* i.e. *hi* is only marked by numeral 1. *Udātta* before *virāma* (pause) is marked by the numeral 2; e.g. (*ṚV* VI.16.1)
1 2 3 2
viśvéṣāṃ h̲itaḥ | (*SV. Pur* 1.1.2) *viśveṣāṃ hitaḥ* | If there are many *udāttas* preceding *virāma*, the first one only is marked
3 2
by numeral 2 and the others are left unmarked; e.g. *citā goḥ* (*Pur*. 458) [not from *ṚV*] 'tā' and 'goḥ' both have *udātta* accent. The first one i.e. 'tā' is marked by 2 and 'goḥ' is unmarked. *Udātta* followed by *anudātta* is marked by numeral
2 3 1 2
2. (*ṚV* VI.16.10) agna̲ ā yā́hi (*SV.Pūr* 1) agna ā yāhi. When *anudātta* follows *udāttas*, the first *udātta* is marked by numeral 2 and the others are left unmarked;

(*ṚV* VIII.6.30) āditpra̲tnasya̲. . .

2u 3 2 3
(*SV Pūr* 20) *ādit pratna sya*. . .

The *svarita* after *udāttas* is marked by the numeral 2ra; e.g. (*ṚV* VIII.64.7). . . *kastam sáparyati* | (*SV Pūr* 142) -

2ra
Kastam saparyati |. The *kṣaipra, jātya, práśliṣta* and *abhinihita* *svaritas* followed by *anudātta, eka - śruti* and *virāma* are marked by 2ra, if *kṣaipra* etc. are not preceded by *udātta* e.g. *kṣaipra* followed by *anudātta* - (*ṚV* VIII. 1.18). . . *ta̱nvā́* *gi̱rā*. . . (*SV* Pūr.52). . .

3ka 2ra 3 2u
tanvā gira. . . etc.

Kṣaipra followed by *ekaśruti* -

(*ṚV* VIII.18.13) nyásmin dadhra̱ ā

2ra 3 1
(*SV U.Arc*. II.2.3) *nyasmin* dadhra ā

Kaispra followed by *virāma*

(*ṚV* VI.51.13). . . du̱rā̱dhyá̱m |

3ka 2ra
(*SV Pūr*. 105). . . du̱rā̱dhya̱m |

Jātya followed by *ekaśruti* - e.g.

(*ṚV* III. 29.2). . . *manu̱ṣyébhiḥ*. . .

3ka 2ra
(*SV Pūr* 79). . . manuṣyebhiḥ. . .

Práśliṣṭa followed by *ekaśruti* - e.g.

(*ṚV* VIII. 98.7) *adhā̱ híndra*. . .

2 3ka 2ra
(*SV Pūr*. 406) adhā hīndra. . .

But this rule of marking with 2ra will not apply if *kṣaipra* etc. are preceded by *udātta*. e.g. (*ṚV* VIII. 45.22) - *tṛ̱mpā*

3 1 2 3
vyáśnuhī; (*SV. Pūr.* 161) tṛmpā vyaśnuhī *Kṣaipra, jātya, prásliṣta* and *abhinihita svaritas* become *pluta* (elongated) when followed by *udātta,* e.g. *kṣaipra* - (*ṚV* VIII.60.9) *pāhyu ita*(*SV Pūr* 36) - *Pāhyū₃ta* (pāhi + uta)

Jātya - (*ṚV* X.115.1) *dūtyamicarán* |; (*SV. Pūr*.64) - *dūtyām3caran*| *abhinihita* - (*ṚV* VIII. 3.1) - *vṛdhe 3ʃ smāṃ avantu*: (*SV. Pūr* 239) - *vṛdhe 3 ʃsmáṃ avantu . .*

The *kṣaipra* etc. when preceded by *udātta* are unmarked e.g. (*ṚV* IX.108.3) *tvam* hyaiṅga; (*SV. Pūr* 583) *tvam hyā3ṅga.*

When there are many *anudāttas*, only the first is marked. e.g. (*ṚV* VII.1.1) *dūredṛśam gṛhapátim*; (*SV. Pūr* 72) *dūredṛśam gṛhapatim* . When *kṣaipra, jātya* and *praśliṣta* marked by 2*ra* are preceded by *anudātta*, this *anudātta* is marked by 3ka. e.g. *kṣaipra-tanvā girā*; *jātya-manuṣyebhiḥ*; *prásliṣta-adhā hīndra.* In the illustration *pāhyū3ta*, *kṣaiprasvarita* is makred without *ra,* hence *anudātta ā* in pā is marked by 3 only. Ekaśruti is left unmarked - e.g. *agna ā yāhi. The vowel i in the syllable hi* of the word *yāhi* is *eka-śruti* and hence unmarked.

In the recitation of the Brāhmaṇas, the two *svaras udātta*

and *anudātta* are employed, the pitches of which would be high and low respectively. These are called *bhāṣikasvaras*. In some recensions *tāna* is given as the *svara* of the Brāhmaṇas. It is called *ekaśrutisvara*. The *Yajus*-formulas were recited with three *svaras* like the *Saṁhitā* or with two *svaras* like the Brāhmaṇa. The Nāradīyásikṣā (1.8.2) states that the *udātta* after *svarita* is called *pracaya*. [The *anudātta* after *svarita* is called *pracaya*; its utterance is similar to that of *udātta*.] The Śikṣā of Yājñavalkya (227, 228) says that the *svarita* is a combination of the *udātta* and the *anudātta*, while *pracaya* is the identification of them. The *ekaśruti* i.e. the *pracaya* is the concealment of the difference between the *udātta* and the *anudātta* like the mixture of milk and water. In the *svarita*, the *udātta* and the *anudātta* are found existing separately. In addition to these four, the Nāradīyásikṣā (1.7.19) gives *nighāta* as the fifth variety of *svara*. Nighāta is that *anudātta svara*, which does not become *pracaya* and hence, retains its place as *anudātta*, when an *udātta* or *svarita* follows it. According to Dr. Sankaran, the enclitic *svarita* in the pre-Vedic period, must have been a middle tone, while the identification of it with the independent circumflex and its consequent rising in its first part, the second part being at the level of *udātta* must have taken place in the historic Vedic period.

(e) The *Yoni* of Sāman and the Sāman

The *ṛc* is the *yoni* i.e. the basis of the *Sāman*. The *ṛc* is marked with the numerals 1, 2 and 3 as explained in the accentuation of *ārcika*. These numerals denote musical pitches. Some changes are effected in the *yoni* for the purpose of chanting. These changes are as follows -

	(Ṛv)	(Sāmagāna)
	1	4
(1) *Vikāra* (modification)	e.g. *agne*	*ognāi* (G.G.G.1)
	(VI.16.10)	
	1	1 -
(2) *Viśleṣaṇa* (disjunction)	e.g. vī̱taye	voitoyāʃ2i
	(VI.16.10)	(G.G.G. 1)
	1	1
(3) *Vikarṣaṇa* (protraction)	e.g. ye	yāʃ2 3 yi
	(*ū̱ī̱*.10.5)	(G.G.G. 98.1)
	1	1 -
(4) *Abhyāsa* (repetition)	e.g. *taye*	toyāʃ2i |
		1
	(VI.16.10)	toyāʃ2i (DD)
		ra 2ra
(5) *Virāma* (pause for	e.g. *gṛṇāno*	gṛ́ṇānoha
the sake of *gāna*	(VI.16.10)	(G.G.G. 98.1)

though there is no word-ending)		1 1 - havyadātaye vyadātoyāꓢ2i (VI.16.10)
(6) *Stobha* (the additional syllables other than those of the text of the *ṛc*	e.g.	*hāu, vā, auhovā* etc.

[see *Śabara* on Jaiminisūtra 9.2.23]

The *āgama* (augmentation) and the *lopa* (disappearance) are also included among these changes -

Āgama - It is the insertion of an extra letter or syllable within a radical word - e.g. *vareṇyam* (*ṚV* III. 62.10) is changed as. . . vareṇiyam (G.G.G.P.1) [1 ra]

Lopa - It is the disappearance of syllable e.g. (*ṚV* III.62.10). . . pracodayát ǀ; (G.G.G. P1) .. ǁ dāyo ǁ ā ꓢ345 ǁ. [1 2 111]

Out of these changes *stobhas* are given in detail in the Stobhānusaṁhāra. *Stobha* according to Jaimini (9.2.11.38) is in addition to the syllables of the *ṛc* and is different from them. (*adhikaṁ ca vivarṇam ca*). The *stobha* is a modification that is applied to the *ṛc* whilst it is joined with the melody. It is of three types - *varṇastobha, padastobha* and *vākyastobha, i, e.* etc. would be illustrations of *varṇastobha, atha, iha* etc. that of *padastobha* and 'aganma joytīḥ ǀ *amṛtā abhūma,* '*namoऽnnāya, namoऽnnapataye* etc. that of *vākyastobha*. The *vākyastobhas* are small phrases containing a thought as per the view of J.M. Vonder Hoogt. The definition given in the commentary by Sāyaṇa is that 'when there is addition, the syllable different from the *ṛc* is *stobha*. (Jaiminīyanyāyamālāvistara 9.2.11 [verse 18]). The word '*varṇa*' (syllable) in the singular, should be understood to denote the group of syllables also to cover the cases of *padastobha* (i.e. the *stobha* in the form of a word) and *vākyastobha* (i.e. the *stobha* in the form of a sentence). Mentioning the view of A.F.H. Strongways and M.S. Ramaswamy Iyer that the *stobhas* are meaningless repetitions. Shri. M.L. Sitaraman opines that 'the *stobhas* are to be looked upon as carefully preserved relics of the musical style of a remote past and must have served the purpose of basic melody at a time when musical instruments as the *yāl* or *vīṇā* still remained to be discovered. He further says that the *stobhas* were the essential feature of the earliest music. "The different *stobhas* must have served the duel purpose of the key and key-notes to be used in a particular *Sāman*." Before the discovery of *vīṇās*, *yāls* and flutes, *stobhas* must have been essential to a concert of *sāmagas* for reproducing the melody in perfect unison. This role of *stobhas* pointed out by Shri Sitaraman needs careful consideration. There is no doubt that the *stobhas* have significance from the musical point of view. But to say that they served the purpose of key-note appears to be a conjecture. The ending of the *Sāman* (i.e. the *nidhana*) was to be chanted by all the three main *Sāman-singers* i.e. the *prastotṛ, udgātṛ* and the *pratihartṛ*. The *upagāna* rendered by the three to six *upagātṛs* in the *mandra* note might have served the purpose of keynote in ancient *Sāman*-singing. The *nidhana* does not consist of *stobha* always. It consisted of the word of the *ṛc* in many cases. It can be said that the *stobhas* in addition to their musical significance, contain the symbolic expression of praise of the deities which were to be pleased by the chanting of *Sāmans*. There are some *Sāmans* which consist of *stobhas* only e.g. *Śāktyasāman* (G.G.G. 156.5), two *Vācovrataṁ-sāmans* (A.G. 167, 168), Vyāhṛtisāman (A.G. serial no. 172) etc. Hillebrandt states that the same stanzas were at times to be chanted to one or various melodies and same melody to various stanzas. Hence it was often necessary to model, to enlarge, to modify the *ṛcs* in correspondence with the *Sāmans* and the creation of that *staubhika* - form developed a technical literature like the Puṣpasūtra. This hypothesis of Hillebrandt about the origin of the *stobhas* is refuted by Hoogt. He says that the *stobhas* did not come into being because a melody of an octosyllabic verse was sung to a twelve syllabic one. In such a case, the same part of the melody was repeated. He states further that the *stobhas* by themselves were no unimportant support of voice; on the contrary a great sacral significance was attached to the mostly meaningless *stobhas*. Faddegon gives the name 'Ritualistic Dadaism' to *stobhas*, specially to the *padastobhas* and the sound (i.e. varṇa) *stobhas*. Dadā 'is the *stobha* on which an entire *Sāman* is built (G.G.G. 156.5). According to Hoogt, it would not be difficult to enumerate a long series of practises through which the Vedic chanter succeeded in turning his *Sāmans* into '*Dadaism.*' He says that the intervening of *Sāmans* with the verses of another *Sāman* necessarily resulted in unintelligibility of both the texts to the mortal auditory.

(f) The Vedic Accents and the Sāman Notes

The word *svara* is used both for the accent and the

musical note. The *svara* of Vedic recitation was of three types namely *udātta* (high), *anudātta* (low) and *svarita* (circumflex). The *tānasvara* was the monotone. In his commentary on the Katyāyana Kāśrautasūtra (1.8.18), Yājñikadeva explains *tāna* as *ekaśruti*. It is the svara of the *mantras*. The *mantras* are to be recited in monotone, devoid of the high and low tones. It is to be so for the other *svaras* are not fixed (*svarāntara* is not *niyata*) while the *śruti* is fixed. On Jaiminisūtra (9.2.8.31) Kumārila says that the traditional mention of the Vedic *svaras* is there for the sake of understanding of the meaning. The *bhāṣikasvara* is the utterance with two pitches only i.e. *udātta* (high) and *anudātta* (low) as in the case of the recitation of the Śatapathabrāhmaṇa.

The Vedic *Traisvarya* —

e.g. *sahasraśīrṣā purúṣaḥ sahasrākṣaḥ sahasrapāt* |
sa bhūmim viśvato vṛtvātyatiṣṭhaddaśāṅgulam ||

(*ṚG.* X.90.1)

Svarita is indicated by vertical line over the syllable and *anudātta* by horizontal line under the syllable. Udātta is left unmarked. One or more than one *anudātta* syllables following the *svarita* are to be uttered similar to the *udātta* syllable and hence are left unmarked. Such *anudātta* syllables are called *pracaya* (a group). The last syllable of this group, when followed by *udātta* or *svarita* is turned into *anudātta*. Yājñikadeva on Kātyāyanaśrautasūtra (1.8.19) states that in the sacrificial procedure the utterance of *mantras* is to be in the *ekaśruti* (monotone). Pracaya, *udāttaśruti* and *ekaśruti* are synonyms. The *pracaya* when followed by *udātta* or *svarita* is rendered as *anudātta*. This is called *nighāta*. Pracaya and *nighāta* appear not to be quite different *svaras* as such, for the utterance of *pracaya* is similar to *udātta* and that of *nighāta* similar to *anudātta*. From the musical point of view, the *udātta, anudātta* and *svarita* are heard in the present practice of Vedic recitation as the notes *Sa, Ni* and *Re* respectively. Nār.Ś (I. 1.1) says that the Āhvarakas employ *tṛtīya, prathama* and *kruṣṭa svaras*. If *prathama* is understood as Ma, these three would correspond to the three pitches identical with the notes Re, Ma and Pa respectively. Taittirīyaprātiśākhya (II.23.17) says that Taittirīyas have *mandra* after *dvitīya* and then *tṛtīya* and *caturtha*. This is called *caturyama*. The commentary on this *sūtra* explains - Mandra i.e. *anudātta* comes after *dvitiya* i.e. *udatta*. Then follow the *tṛtīya* and *caturtha* i.e. *pracaya* and *svarita* respectively. Thus the four *yamas* (i.e. *svaras*) are there in order. The group of these four *yamas* is the *caturyama*. Hence there are four *svaras* only in the Taittirīyaśākhā. The Tai-Prā (1-4 to 45) states in regard to *svarita* that the beginning part of it is *udāttatara* immediately after *udātta*, for half a *mātrā*. Then the remaining part is similar to *udātta* or *anudāttatara* (i.e. lower than *anudātta*) or similar to *anudātta*. The musical equivalence of these four pitches would be Re, Sa, Dha and Ni. Nār.Ś gives the four stages of *svara* employment as *ārcika, gāthika, sāmika* and *svarāntara*. In the Bṛhaddeśī (p. 17) we find the explanation of these terms. The employment of one tone (i.e. monotone) is called *ārcika*, that of two tones *gāthika*, of three tones *sāmika* and of four tones *svarāntara*. Nār.Ś. (I.7.19) mentions the five-fold *svara* as *udātta, anudātta, svarita, pracita* (i.e. pracaya) and *nighāta*. This same śikṣā (I.8.2) states that *pracaya* is not a different *svara* as it is identical with *udātta*. Nighāta is the *anudātta* which does not remain as *pracaya* and is rendered as *anudātta*, when an *udātta* or *svarita* follows.

Sāman Notes

The Puṣpasūtra (IX.26) states that the Kauthumas sing the majority of *Sāmans* with five notes, some with six notes and only two with seven notes. Thus the pentatonic, hexatonic and heptatonic employment of notes is clearly given by the PS. Aitareyabrāhmaṇa (7.7) states that speech is expressed in seven-fold manner. In the commentary Sāyaṇa says that the speech in the form of *gāna* (singing) preceded in a seven-fold manner endowed with the notes *ṣadja, ṛsabha* etc. in regard to the popular practice and endowed with the notes *kruṣṭa, prathama, dvitīya* etc. in regard to Vedic practice. The Ṛkprātiśākhya (13.17) states that there are seven *yamas* of speech. These *yamas* are the seven notes. The next *Sūtra* (13.18) says 'or they should be understood differently.' This *Sūtra* is explained by Uvaṭa as there are different *yamas* among these notes. Sāyaṇa explains it as they should be understood to be different from *ṣadja* etc. namely *kruṣṭa* etc. According to him, this *Sūtra* is concerned with the different names of the notes as stated in the popular and Vedic music. Bharatasvamin also follows him. If Uvaṭaś explanation is relied upon, it would indicate the intermediate *svara* positions.

Yama, literally means 'restraining' or 'controlling' from *yam* meaning to restrain or control. The *yamas* are the controlled pitch-expressions of the speech. The word *yama* also means a twin. Thus the manifestation of a note in close proximity with the note proper can be also indicated by the word *yama*. This would lead to the concept of *'sruti* used by Nārada in regard to the manifestation of notes. The commentator of Taittirīy-aprātiśākhya, while commenting on the Sūtra 13.16 explains that in the Sāmaveda the note *tṛtīya* is the basis from which there are three notes in ascending order (*utkṣepins*) and three in descending order (*avakṣepins*). That means *dvitīya, prathama* and *kruṣṭa* would be gradually in the ascending order from the *tṛtīya* and the *caturtha, mandra* and *atisvārya* would be gradually in descending order. The *tṛtīya* note would be called *dhṛta pracaya* as it is sustained. It is the middle note among the seven notes of *Sāman*-music.

The Vaidika names of the *Sāman*-notes are found in the S.V. Br. first. They are - *kruṣṭatama, prathama, dvitīya, tṛtīya, caturtha, pañcama* and *antya* or *ṣaṣṭha*. From the commentary of Sāyaṇa *kruṣṭatama* seems to be the highest note in the *Sāman*-scale which is not different from *kruṣṭa*, for while giving the deities of the *svaras* this name *kruṣṭa* is only mentioned. *Kruṣṭa* belongs to Prajāpati, Brahman or Viśvedevas, *prathama* to Āditya, *dvitīya* to Sādhyas, *tṛtīya* to Agni, *caturtha* to Vāyu, *mandra* (i.e. *pañcama*) to Soma and *antya* (i.e. *atisvārya*) to Mitrā-Varuṇā. The Bṛhaddevatā gives the name of the fifth note as *mandra* and of the sixth as *atisvāra* or *atisvārya*. The Sāmatantra does not include *antya* among the principal *svaras*. That means the six notes beginning from *kruṣṭa* and ending with *mandra* can be *prakṛti svaras* while *atisvārya* can be only *vikṛtisvara*. Bṛhaddevatā says that the note *atisvārya* is endowed with the *karṣaṇa* (pulling) of *mandra*. Thus as *atisvārya* depends upon *mandra* it is never an independent note. This seems to be the reason behind the statement of Sāmatantra which does not admit *antya* among the *svaras* of *Sāman*. In the Sāmatantra the syllables *gi, ji, ḍi, di, bi* denote the ntoes *prathama, dvitīya, tṛtīya, caturtha* and *pañcama* respectively. As the note *kruṣṭa* is rare, it seems that it is not included among the regular notes.

The Nār.Ś. gives the descending order of the *Sāman* notes beginning from *kruṣṭa* and ending with *atisvārya*. He has stated the *gātravīṇā* indications of these notes as follows :

kruṣṭa is to be indicated at the top part of the thumb and *prathama* at the thumb. The remaining notes are to be indicated by touching the tip of the thumb to the middle part of the fingers i.e. *gāndhāra* (*dvitīya*) by touching the middle part of the index finger, *ṛṣabha* (*tṛtīya*) by touching the middle part of the middle finger, *ṣaḍja* (*caturtha*) by touching the middle part of the ring finger, *dhaivata* (*mandra*) by touching the middle part of the little finger and *niṣāḍa* (*atisvārya*) by touching the base of the little finger. The thumb is kept two *yavas* apart (i.e. approximately 1/8") to indicate *kruṣṭa* in the Kauthuma tradition. To indicate the *prathamasvara*, it is kept one *yava* apart. In the Bhūmikā (Introduction) of the Sāmavedīyarudrajapavidhi, it is stated that the *kruṣṭasvara* is indicated by keeping the thumb up and the *prathamasvara* by keeping it on the middle of the forefinger. The *prathamasvara* is identified with *gāndhāra*, so the *kruṣtasvara* has to be identified with the *madhyama* note. The *Nāradīyaśikṣā* (1.7.5) has the name *parisvāra* also in the place of *atisvārya*. In the Sāmatantra, the combination of *atisvārya, mandra* and *atisvārya* is called *parisvāra*.

Nāradīyaśikṣā (1.5.12) states the identification of the

sāmasvaras and those of the *svaras* produced from flute (i.e.the notes in popular music) as follows:

The *prathamasvara* of the *Sāman*-chanters is the *madhyama* note of the *veṇu*, the *dvitīya* is the *gāndhāra, tṛtīya* is *ṛṣabha, caturtha* is *ṣaḍja*, the *pañcama* is *dhaivata*, the *ṣaṣṭha* is *niṣāda* and the seventh is *pañcama.* The scale of *Sāman* notes is descending. Hence, the order of these *Sāman*-notes would start from the *madhyama* note and end on the *pañcama* note. The commentator Bhaṭṭaśobhākara explains the word *veṇu* as a flute. Later, while giving the positions of the notes in the *gātra-vīṇā* (1.7.3, 4) it is stated that the *kruṣṭa* note is to be indicated by the tip (i.e. the upperpart of the thumb), the *prathama* note by the thumb, *gāndhāra* on the forefinger, then *ṛṣabha* on the middle, the *ṣadja* on the ring finger, *dhaivata* on the little finger and below it at the base the *niṣāda* note. This description gives the *Sāman*-scale as *kṛusṭa, prathama* etc. (i.e. Ma, Ga, Ri, Sa, Dha, Ni). While commenting on 1.5.2, Bhaṭṭaśobhākara says that *kruṣṭa* is the seventh note *pañcama.* The note Pa would be the lowest as per the description. But then it is difficult to identify *kruṣṭa* with the lowest note *pañcama*. The meaning of *kruṣṭa* points out that it is the highest note in the *Sāman*-scale (The word *kruṣṭa* is derived from the root *kruś* meaning 'to yell'). Hence there is difficulty in understanding the exact identification of *kruṣṭa*.

(g) The Notational Systems of Sāman Chants

[1] *Numeral Notation*

In the published texts of Kauthumasāmagāna, the notes are indicated by the numbers. Numbers 1 to 5 occurring on the syllables of the *gāna* are the primary numbers. The note *kruṣṭa* is indicated by the number 1 put twice i.e. by 11. Numbers 1 to 6 appear in the textual line itself. They indicate the secondary position of the notes. Number 7 over the syllable stands for the *abhigītasvara* in Kauthuma tradition. The number 6 never comes at the beginning of the *Sāman*. Kruṣṭa never occurs at the beginning and at the end of the *Sāman*. Its occurrence is very rare. It is found in the G.G.G.284.2 and Káśyapavrataanugāna first (A.G. 141.1). Numbers 1 to 6 coming in the line of the syllables denote grace notes or glides and form decorative phrases. The difference between the notes denoted by the primary numbers and the secondary appears to be that the former are employed while pronouncing the syllables while latter are used as *ālāpa*. The *kruṣṭa* and other six notes were called *yamas*. The Ṛkprātiśākhya (13-17) states that the seven notes are *yamas*. The expression '*pṛthagvā*' is explained by Sāyaṇa as 'or other than *kruṣṭa*' etc. i.e. *Ṣadja* etc. The tones which are very close to each other are not recognised distinctly as separate ones easily. (The word *yama* means twin also.) Hence, the *yamas* are the seven notes with the proper intervals between one another. The Puṣpasūtra gives the *Sāman* scale as *kruṣṭādi*, which can be understood from the concept of *udūha* stated in it later on as *kruṣṭa, prathama, dvitīya, tṛtīya, caturtha, mandra* and *atisvārya*. Mandra is called *pañcama* (i.e. fifth) and *atisvārya, ṣaṣṭha* (sixth) or *antya* (coming at the end).

The inversion of the descending order i.e. *sa, dha, ni* in place of *sa, ni, dha,* seems to be due to the shaky position of the *pracaya*. The Bṛhaddevatā (8.116-120) mentions the seven notes *kruṣṭa* etc. as connected with head, palate, the middle part of the eye-brows, ear and the tip of nose respectively. The *mandra* is a chest-note. The *atisvārya* is the protraction of the *mandra*. The Nāradīyaśikṣā gives the names of the *Sāman*-scale in a different order also (1.1.12) - namely, *prathama, dvitīya, tṛtīya, caturtha, mandra, kruṣṭa* and *atisvārya.* In this gamut, *kruṣṭa* is the sixth note in the descent. The Sāmavidhānabrāhmaṇa states that *kruṣṭa* is the highest note. The mention of notes in the Bṛhaddevatā places *kruṣṭa* higher than *prathama.* The Sāmatantra employs syllables *gi, ji, ḍi, di* and *bi* for the notes *prathama, dvitīya, tṛtīya, caturtha* and *mandra* respectively. Its first *Sūtra* is *svaronantyaḥ.* The commentary mentions, *kruṣṭa,* first and then illustrates the *parvans* in which *prathama, dvitīya, tṛtīya, caturtha* and *pañcamasvara* occurs. That means it does not recognise the *antya svara* i.e. the *atisvārya*-note in the series of the notes of the *Sāman*-scale. This non-mention might be due to the unimportant position of *atisvārya,* as it never occurs at the beginning of the *Sāman* and on the syllable and hence it is not a main note. The Sāmaparibhāṣā identifies the *kruṣṭā di* series with the notes Ni, Dha, Pa, Ma, Ga, Ri and Sa respectively. The word *kṛṣṭa* is found in the commentary on the *Sūtra* no. 405 occurring in the fourth *prapāṭhaka* of the Sāmatantra. In the explanation of the *sūtra-'kruṣṭām ji migoḥ,'* the variant reading *kṛṣṭa* is seen in the foot-note 6 of the commentary. Accepting this variant reading some scholars justify the position of Pa as the lowest note in the *Sāman*-scale starting from Ma which would be the highest *Sāman*-note and hence identified as the first note in the descending scale. But understanding the highest note as Pa, the other scholars identify *kruṣṭa* with Pa, from which the descending *Sāman*-scale starts. The Saṁhitopaniṣadbrāhmaṇa (3.2) states the concept of *udūha* according to which the *caturtha*, the *mandra* and the *atisvārya* notes are pronounced higher by the intermediate two notes; i.e. the syllable having the *caturtha svara* is pronounced as having *prathamasvara*, the one having *mandrasvara* is pronounced as having *dvitīyasvara* and the one having *atisvāryasvara* as having *tṛtīyasvara*. This procedure is to be employed only before the *upāya*, i.e. the statement which is in proximity to *nidhāna* having *mandrasvara*. In the chanting of the *stotra*, there are three *udgātṛs*. The part which is to be chanted by the three together is the *nidhana*. That means the *nidhana* having the *caturtha, mandra* and *atisvārya* notes is not to have *udūha*.

The musical notes are indicated by the numerals 1 to 7. The first note indicated by the numeral 1 in the series of the numerals 1 to 7 would be the highest note. This note is the *kruṣṭa* in the *Kruṣṭādi*-series. The correspondence by taking Pa or Ma as the *kruṣṭasvara* the two series can be stated as follows :

(1)	Pa	Ma	Ga	Ri	Sa	Ni	Dha
	Kruṣṭa	1	2	3	4	Mandra	*atisvārya*
(2)	Ma	Ga	Ri	Sa	Ni	Dha	Pa
	Kruṣṭa	1	2	3	4	*mandra*	*atisvārya*

If Pa in the second series is understood as *Kṛṣṭasvara*

(3) The series would be understood as :

Ma	Ga	Ri	Sa	Ni	Dha	Pa
1	2	3	4	5	6	*kṛṣṭa*

The numeral 7 is understood in the Kauthuma tradition as denoting the sequence *abhigīta*. According to the statement of Nāradīyaśikṣā, there is the inversion of the descending order in regard to Sa, Dha, Ni which might be due to the *śākhā-bheda* (the difference in the chants of a particular school, which the śikṣā has followed). It is rather difficult to understand the correspondence of the *kruṣṭādi* series with the *niṣādādi*-series. Kallinātha, while commenting on the Saṁgītaratnākara (I.1.25) says that the *Sāman*-notes *kruṣṭa, prathama* etc. have the names *ṣaḍja* etc. suitably. This view of Kallinātha appears to have been based on the modern practice of music in which the seven notes beginning with *ṣaḍja* end in the note *Niṣāda*, in the appropriate order. The same *svara*, when secures the position of another *svara* gets the appellation *visvara* e.g. *o*[1]*ʃ2345i*. In this illustration the letter *o*[1] having the *prathamasvara* is pulled in the descending order (*kṛṣṭa*) to the note denoted by the numeral 5 (i.e. *mandra* note). The *visvara* is found in the *pratutkrama, atikrama, karṣaṇa*, and *svāra* as per the Mātrālakṣaṇa. It gets the time measure of 3 *mātrās* in each *svara*.

(1) Pratutkrama - It is of the nature of ascent. It is stated to be of nine kinds :

(i) *atisvārya* ascends to *mandra* - e.g. . . dāʃ656m|; (G.G.G. 23.2) Kayā[3 2] ʃ3 sthā[4] ʃ 5 yirā ʃ656n| (G.G.G.13.1) etc.

(ii) *mandra* ascends to the *caturtha* - e.g. . . vidā[5]ʃ4 dvāsūm; (G.G.G. 237.4); purojitī[5 ra]vo[ra]ʃ4ndhāʃ[5]āḥ etc. (G.G. G. 545.6);

(iii) *caturtha* ascends to tṛtīya - e.g. dutā[5ra 4]ʃ3m (G.G.G. 12.1); devo[5ra 4]ʃ3 (G.G.G. 55.1); mānā[5ra 4]ʃ3 (G.G.G.128.2);

(iv) *tṛtīya* ascends to *dvitīya* - gi[3]ʃ234rā[5]ḥ (G.G.G. 34.1); hī[3]ʃ234ṣ[5]ī (G.G.G. 1.1);

2ra 2ra1

(v) *dvitīya* ascends to *prathama* - auhoʃri agne... (G.G.G.5.2)

2

dṛśesʃi (G.G.G. 10.1);

(vi) *mandra* ascends to tṛtīya in *sandhi* passing over the

5ra ra 5ra 2 3 5

caturtha - ·· somapā | āvnāoʃ234vā (G.G.G. 285.2);

5 3 2

[somapā*vne*]; imamindra. . . (G.G.G. 344.2)

(vii) *mandra* ascends to *dvitīya*, passing over *caturtha* and

4 5 [4] 5

tṛtīya - abhi priyā ʃ2 (G.G.G. 554.2); ṣibhā ʃ2 u (G.G.G. 559.2);

(viii) *tṛtīya* ascends to *prathama* passing over *dvitīya* -

3 2

punāʃ31 (G.G.G. 511.16);

(ix) *mandra* ascends to *prathama* passing over *caturtha*,

1ra 2ra 3ra 2

tṛtīya and *dvitīya* - ī5hī hī hī hī hī (A.G. 103.1)

The case no. (ix) is not given in the Mātrālakṣaṇa. For the *pratutkrama*, the appellation *nu* is stated in the Sāmatantra.

(2) Atikrama: It is of four types. In it the note or notes in between are omitted in the descending order:

11

(i) *kruṣṭa* — ū ʃ 2 (G.G.G. 254.2);

(ii) *prathama* — descends to *tṛtīya* crossing over dvitīya -

1ra na 2 1 na

āroʃ 3 hān (G.G.G. 92.1); māsīʃ3yā (G.G.G. 176.1);

The syllable *na* over the syllable of the *ṛc* denotes *namanasvara* which is identical with *prathamasvara*.

(iii) *tṛtīya* descends to *mandra*, crossing over *caturtha* -

4 3
yajñā ʃ5 ya (G.G.G. 35.4).

(iv) *prathama* - descends to *mandra* crossing over *dvitīya*,

1 1 2ra 3ra 2
tṛtīya and *caturtha* - e.g. īʃ 5 hī hī hī hi hī (A.G. 181) in the Aśvinorvratasāman.

(3) Karṣaṇa (pulling) is of five types :

1
(i) *prathama* pulled down to *dvitīya* - bodhāʃ2 (G.G.G. 15.1);

1 2
(ii) *prathama* pulled down to *tṛtīya* - āʃ23indrāḥ (G.G.G. 275.2);

1
(iii) *prathama* pulled down to *caturtha* - āʃ 234 (G.G.G.

1
275.2); nmāʃ234bhāi (G.G.G. 8.7.1);

1
(iv) *prathama* pulled down to *mandra* - oʃ2345 (G.G.G. 3.1)

5 5
(v) *mandra* pulled down to *atisvārga* - tvaṃtvāʃ6me (G.G.G. 42.2);

(4) Svāra - It begins with numeral one, numeral two and numeral three and ends in numeral 5. It is of three kinds:

1 111
(i) oʃ23451 (G.G.G. 32.1);

2 111
(ii) vāʃ345 (G.G.G. 35.4);

1 3 111
(iii) upāʃ2345 (G.G.G. 36.3)

(5) Vinata - It begins with the *prathama* and ends on *dvitīya*

1 vi
- āindroꞅ2 (G.G.G. 290.1)

(6) Praṇata - It begins with *dvitīya* and ends on *tṛtīya*

2 ra ^ 1
- tigmena ꞅ 3 śo (G.G.G. 22.1)

(7) Utsvarita - It begins with *caturtha* and ends on *mandra*

4
- hoꞅ5i (G.G.G. 41.1).

(8) Abhigīta - It begins with *dvitīya* and ends on *prathama*.

It is indicated by numeral 7 or *a* placed on the syllable e.g.

[1]ra a 4
(G.G.G. 15.2) - stomāꞅṁrūdrā23yā ।

1 a
(G.G.G. 109.1) — oootāindadhāꞅ23 ।

The syllable *na* which is found on the syllable of the chant indicates the *namanasvara* i.e. the note-sequence of the nature, primary numeral 1, then secondary numeral 3 and again primary numeral 2.

1 ra ra 2
($\underline{1}_3\underline{2}$) e.g. āśvoīꞅ3yā (G.G.G. 156.3)

This sequence might be called a specific form of *atikrama*. The *preṅkhasvara* is found on the numeral 2 indicated by a horizontal tone over it or in some South Indian MSS, the syllable *pre*. It is of two types beginning with numeral 1 and 2; e.g. to[1]yāꞅ$\bar{2}$i (G.G.G. 1.7);

[2]
mātauꞅ$\bar{2}$ (G.G.G. 128.2).

The *Sāman* was sung with *samāvartana* which means repetition often. It was performed with *roha* preceding. Roha literally means ascent. When the *madhyama* note is chanted first and then the *gāndhāra* note is sung, this *gāndhāra* is *rohapūrva.* The commentator of Saṁhitopaniṣadbrāhmaṇa states that the *karṣaṇa* from the *dvitiyasvara* to the *caturthasvara* is also called *roha.* The adjective '*vinardi*' occurs in regard to the *Sāman* in the Chāndogyopaniṣad (2.22.1). It is explained by Śāṅkarācārya as follows: '*Vinardi viśiṣṭaḥ nardaḥ svaraviśeṣaḥ ṛṣabhakūjitasamaḥ asya asti,*' in the case of *vinardi gānam.* (The chanting in a particular *svara* similar to the sound of the bull). When in the third foot, the 13 *okāras* are employed in the *dvitīya svara* and 3 *okāras* having the duration of 3 *mātrās* each, are uttered, it is called *nyūṅkha.* When the first syllable of the third foot is uttered with *anudāttasvara* and the second with *udāttasvara*, it is called *ninarda.*

In the morning *savana*, the low (i.e. *mandra*) *svara* should be employed, in the mid-day *savana* medium (*madhyama*) *svara* and in the *tṛtīya savana*, high *svara* (i.e. *kruṣṭa svara*).

[2] *The Syllabic Notation Systems of Sāman Chants*

Syllabic Notation

The old Kauthumagāna manuscripts have the syllabic notation. It is called *prācīna paddhati* or *paribhāṣāpāṭha*. In this system the syllables *ka, ca, ṭa, ta* and *pa* are employed to indicate the *prathama, dvitīya, tṛtīya, caturtha* and *mandra* notes respectively. The syllables *la, va* and *kva* are included in the *ka-class*; *śa, ṣa, sa, śca, ra* and *ḷa* in the *ca*-class; *ya* in the *ṭa*-class and *ha* in the *ta*-class. The consonants of each class are employed with the vowels such as *a, ā, i* , *ī* etc. to indicate the different *parvans*. The five main divisions of the *Sāman* are called *bhaktis*. Each *bhakti* is further divided into parts called *parvans*. The *parvans* in the 5 syllabic classes number as follows:

Those having *prathamasvara* at the beginning - Ka-class: The five syllables of this class namely, *ka, kha, ga, gha* and *ṅa* used with 12 vowels *a, ā, i, ī, u, ū, e, ai, o, au, aṃ* and *aḥ* indicate 60 *parvans*; *la* and *va* with 12 vowels indicate 24 *parvans* and *kva* with the vowels *a, ā, i, ī, u, ū, e* and *ai*, 8 parvans. The total *parvans* indicated by the *ka*-class number 92. The *Ca*-class with 12 vowels indicates 60 *parvans*, *śa, sa, ṣa* 36 *parvans*, śca with vowels (dropping *i*) *a, ā, ī, u, ū, e* = 6; *ra* with the 12 vowel = 12; *ḷa* with the vowels *a, ā, i, ī* = 4 = total 118;

Ṭa-class - Ṭa and ṭha with the 12 vowels 24; ḍa with the vowels *a, ā, i, ī, u, ū, e, ai, o* and *au* = 10; *ya* with the vowels *a, ā, i, ī, u, ū, ai, o, au, aṁ, aḥ* = 11 (excluding the vowel *e* = 45).

Ta-class - *ta* with 12 vowels = 12; *tha* with the vowels *a, ā, i, ī, u, ū, e* and *ai* = 8; *ha* wth the vowels *a, ā* and *ī* = 3 total 23.

Pa-class - *pa* with the 12 vowels = 12 and *pha* with the vowels *a, ā, i, ī, u, ū, e* and *ai* = 8 = 20.

The total number of *parvans* taken together comes to 298. The *parvan* having *kruṣṭa* note is a single syllable *parvan* namely ū^{11}. (Number 1 is used twice to indicate *kruṣṭa*). With
3 ra 1 ra
the syllabic notation it is indicated as *ūkaka*. Following are a few illustrations of *parvans* with numeral and syllabic notation:

3 ra
(i) kāꭍ5yā I ū́ - kāṭaṁiyā I ūka - in this syllabic notation ṭa indicates *tṛtīya*-note, *mi* indicates *atikrama* and ka
1
indicates *prathama* note.

2
(ii) ṣṭhayauhoꭍ3 I - *ṣṭhaṭi* yauho - *ṭi* indicates *tṛtīya* note.

(iii) hi[1]mmāʃ2-hikāmmāpre-kā indicates *prathama* note, *pre* indicates *preṅkha* etc. There is no indication of *svara* in regard to the *stobha* in the illustration no (ii).

This syllabic notation is complicated. There is the possibility of the notational syllables being understood as the textual syllables. Hence the published Kauthuma texts have followed the numerical notation. Among the three Sāmaveda schools available at present, the Rāṇāyanīya syllabic notation is similar to the *prācīnapāṭha* of the Kauthumas. But the Jaiminīya-school of the Tamilnadu *Sāman*-chanters differs in regard to the syllabic notation. It follows the text Dhāraṇalakṣaṇa of Sabhāpati. According to it there are 32 *svaras*. The Sāman-chanters of Kaḍuntarapuḷḷi, who belong to the Jaiminīya school give the following information in regard to these thirty-two *svara* distinctions. There are 16 single and 16 combined *svaras*. The single *svaras* are denoted by the syllables *ka, kha, ca, ṭa, ṇa, ta, tha, pa, pha, bha, ya, sa, pla, ṅa, tra* and *kru*. The combined *svaras* are denoted by the syllables - *ga, gha, cha, ja, jha, ṭha, ḍa, ḍha, da, dha, la, na, va, ha, la* and *ba*. These syllables are placed over the syllables of the text. While the syllables indicating notation of the

Kauthuma Rāṇāyanīya tradition are placed after the textual syllables in their line. These 32 *svaras* are indicated by hand-positions called *kai-lakṣaṇas*. A few examples are given here to have some idea. *Ṭa* is shown by the hand held side ways, thumb kept on top and is then cast downwards towards the singer's right. The name of this *svara* is *yāna*. Kru denotes *kruṣṭa svara* and is shown by the hand held side ways, thumb kept on top, the fingers are drawn inwards, except for the index finger. This finger is moved upwards and then downwards. Ya indicates *marśanasvara*. It is shown by the hand held with the palm turned upwards and fingers slightly bent. Then the thumb is moved slowly across the finger tips, starting with the index finger. Gha indicates the combined *svarayānamarśana*. Ga indicates the *svara avaroha-kṣepaṇa; va, avarohāvarta, dha kṣepaṇa marśana*. Jha-*āvartakṣepaṇa* etc. The syllable *śa* indicates the absence of *svara* and comes always after the *svara*-symbol; *ṣa* also denotes the absence of *svara* and it appears before the *svara*-symbol. The Nambudiri Jaiminīyas of Kerala use *kampa* mainly in their chant. Only three principal tones are heard. The central pitch is prominent and the upper and the lower tones are heard in the *vibrato*. This tradition is strictly oral. They employ hand movements called *kaikaṭṭuka* (i.e. hand showing) which are different from those used in the other schools. There are some movements which are obligatory and some optional.

In the numeral notation, the secondary numerals indicating the *āvāntara svaras* are shown in the *gātra viṇā* of Kauthuma tradition as per the Sāmavedīyarudra-Japavidhi, as follows:

Abhigīta : The thumb is taken up from the base of the index finger to its top.

Vinata: The thumb is moved touching the middle part of the index, middle, ring and little fingers.

Praṇata: The thumb is moved from the base of the index finger to its top and stopped there.

Utsvarita: The thumb is moved over the tops of the four fingers.

According to Nārāyaṇasvāmi (Introduction to the Svādhyāyamandal edition of Grāmageyagānam - Araṇyegeya-gānam, 1942) - the following is shown in the *gātraviṇā* of Kauthumas as follows:

Abhigīta: Starting the thumb from the forepart of the index finger and ending at the thumb.

Vinata: The thumb is moved starting from the top of the index finger and ending in the middle part.

Praṇata: Beginning from the index finger and ending on the middle finger.

Utsvarita: Starting from the ring finger and ending on the little finger.

The syllables over which there is no numeral have the *svara* that is indicated by the numeral placed on the syllable preceding it. The long syllable over which *ra* or *o* is placed is to be uttered having the duration of two *mātrās*. The short syllable has the duration of one *mātrā*. The remaining long syllables have the duration of three *mātrās* each. These long syllables are called *vṛddha* ones. In the *vṛddha* syllable the short syllable gets the addition of two *mātrās* and the long one, of one *mātrā*. In the case of *svāra*, the numeral 1 is placed on the numerals indicating the musical notes. This numeral 1 indicates that the note is to be pronounced as having the duration of one *mātrā*. Nāradīyaśikṣā (1.7.10-12) has described the *śrutis* in the case of the notes of the *Sāman* chants. The *mandra, dvitīya, caturtha, atisvārya* and *tṛtīya* have *dīptā śṛuti* and *kruṣṭa* has *karuṇā*. The commentator says that these five have *dīptā, prathama* has *mṛdu* and the seventh (i.e. *kruṣṭa*) has *karuṇā*. The *dvitīya* (i.e. Gāndhāra) has another three *śrutis* namely *mṛdu, madhyā* and *āyatā*. The nature of *āyatā* is effected when the low note follows the *dvitīya*, and that of *mṛdu* when there is inversion (*viparyaya*). When the same note follows, there is the middle nature (*madhyamatva*) (verses 11 and 12). The commentator explains that when the low note i.e. *tṛtīya* follows the *dvitīya*, the *śruti* is *āyata* (extended); when there is inversion i.e. *caturtha* note follows *dvitīya*, the *śruti* is *mṛdu* (soft) and when the same note follows i.e. *dvitīya* follows *dvitīya*, the *śruti* effected is *madhyamā*. So the distinction between these three *śrutis* of *dvitīya* is based on its utterance which is affected by the following note. (Abhinavagupta, explaining this text which occurs in the description of the embellishment *veṇi* in the Nāṭyaśāstra, Ch. 29) says that when *Gāndhāra* is followed by Ṛṣabha, the *śruti* is *āyatā*, when it is followed by the note *madhyama*, the *śruti* is *mṛdu* and when the note *Gāndhāra* is followed by the note *Gāndhāra*, the *śruti* is *madhyā*. He takes *viparyaya* (inversion) to mean higher note following the *dvitīya*. The word *śruti* is understood here as the particular manner of pronouncing the note, brilliantly, softly and pathetically etc. Thus the concept of *śruti* is connected with the note-manifestation. In the published Kauthuma text of Sāmagāna, the sign '^' occurs over the syllable denoting the *āyatāśruti*. It is effected when the numeral 2 indicating *dvitīya* is followed by the numeral 3 indicating *tṛtīya*. Dīptā is indicated by the sign $\hat{1}$. There is no sign seen in the MSS for *mṛdu* and *madhyā*. Karuṇā is the *śruti of kruṣṭa*. It is as stated above by the sign 11 over the syllable.

The unit of time-measure is *mātra*. It is metrical time-unit. The short syllable is of one *mātrā* duration, the long syallable of two *mātrā* duration is indicated by the sign *ra* or *o* over it, the other long syllables have the duration of three *mātrās*. The Sāmavedins employ the left hand to indicate 1ra to 5ra placed above the syllable in the following manner - 1ra is indicated by the little finger bending it so as to touch the palm;

2ra is shown in this way by the ring finger; 3ra by the middle finger, 4ra by the index finger and 5ra by the thumb placing it on the index finger and closing the fist and opening the fist and again closing it in the said order (Sāmavedīyarudrajapavidhi, Introduction, p.16).

The *avagraha* (ऽ) placed after the syllable indicates that the preceding primary note is to be continued. It can also indicate *atikrama*. The Taittirīyaprātiśākhya (I.41 to 45) states in regard to the time-measure of *svarita*, that its first half *mātrā* is higher than *udātta* (udāttatara) and the remaining part, similar to *udātta* (udāttasama), or lower than *anudātta* (anudāttatara) or similar to *anudātta* (anudāttasama). This four-fold utterance of the *svarita* has significance in regard to the establishment of the 4th note, developed from the *traisvarya* (three notes - *udātta, anudātta* and *svarita* of the Ṛgveda).

(h) The Measure of Time

The Mātrālakṣaṇa speaks of the measure of time-units (*mātrā*) expected to be employed in the chants. These are *hrasva* (short), dīrgha (long), and *pluta* and *vṛddha* (prolated). The short syllable has the duration of one *mātrā*, the long one two *matrās*, and the prolated, three *mātrās*. The short syllable when joined with two *mātrās* and thus making the syllable having the duration of three *mātrās* is called *pluta*; while the long syllable combined with one *mātrā* is termed *vṛddha*. The time-measure is of one-fourth *mātrā*, half *mātrā*, *mātrā*, one and half *mātrās*, two *mātrās*, two and half *mātrās*, three *mātrās*, and three and half *mātrās*. The last one occurs in the case of *ōm*. The measure of one-fourth *mātrā* is called *aṇumātrā*.

Vṛtti (the mode of chanting) is stated to be three-fold in the Nāradīyaśikṣā (1.6.21). The fast (*druta*) while studying, medium (*madhyama*) in the application (in the sacrificial performance) and slow (*vilambita*) in the case of teaching the pupils. The Mātrālakṣaṇa also states these three *vṛttis* (tempo) - fast, moderate and slow. It says, in addition, that in the *druta* the *mātrā* has three *kalās*, in the *madhyama* it has four *kalās* and in the *vilambita*, it has five *kalās*. (The dictionary meaning of *kalā* is the duration of one minute or forty-eight seconds or eight seconds).

(In the musical parlance the duration of a *mātrā* is the time required for five short syllables. But the word *mātrā* in the Vedic sense denotes only the duration of the short syllable).

(i) The Bhāvas Treated in the Puṣpasūtra

The Puṣpasūtra after explaining the various *bhāvas* (modifications) states that all the schools of Sāmaveda should chant the *Sāmans* following the school to which they belong after taking into consideration the modifications - namely,

(1) *āitva* (becoming *āi*) - the *tālavyas* (palatal vowels) in the *ṛc*, which have secured the state of being *vṛddha* in the chant, are changed to *āi*. [These vowels are *i, ī, e* and *ai*]

5 ra 2
e.g. *uccāte* becomes *uccātāʃ3i*. . . in the *Sāman* Āmahīyava (Ūha Daśa1); similarly, in the same *Sāman*, *divi* becomes
21
divāi. . . .

(2) *prakṛti* — [These *vṛddha* syllables are not changed into *āi* but remain in their *vṛddha* state i.e. they are uttered having the duration of three *mātrās* e.g. in the Yaudhājayasāman (Ūha Daśa 3) the syllable *de* of *devo* in the second *stotrīyā* remains without being changed
2
into *āi* - deʃ3vō].

The *tālavya* which has not secured the state of being *vṛddha* remains as it is - e.g. in the *Sāman* Āmahīyava
2 1 2 -
(Ūha Daśa 1), in the *parvan* divāisāʃ1dbhūʃ2, the vowel *i* of *di* has not changed into *āi* as it is not *vṛddha*.

(3) *vṛddha* - the short or long syllable of *ṛc* gets the duration of three *mātrās*. Sometimes the short syllable getting the duration of three *mātras* is called *pluta*. In the Puṣpasūtra the term *vṛddha* is used in both the cases - e.g. in the
2 4
Yaudhājayasāman (Ūha Daśa 3) e.g. nāʃ 3ʃʃ0 the long

syllable *so* of *soma* has secured the duration of three *mātrās*.

(4) *avṛddha* - the syllable expected to be *vṛddha* remains sometimes without being *vṛddha* e.g. Yaudhājayasāman (Ūha. Ekāha 380) — pratnā[3]ʃ[2]31m | pī[2]ʃ3 *yū*[4ra]; Saubhara-sāman (Ūha. Satra 737) e.g. yenā[5ra]ʃ[4]3jyo[2]ʃ3*tī*[4ra].

The fourth syllables in these *Sāmans* namely *Yū* and *tī* respectively have not become *Vṛddha*.

(5) *gata* or *gati* - the chanting of the word ending in *i* or *u* ('*igati*' or '*ugati*') e.g. hāi, hāu.

(6) *agata* - the *gati i* or *u* is elided - e.g. in the Vāmrasāman (Ūha Daśa 87) the latter *stobha hoi* has its *i* elided — adhā[1]ho̅ʃ2il ṣṇubhā[1]irho̅ʃ2.

(7) *ucca* - the syllable having low *svara* in the *ṛc* is chanted in high *svara* in the *gāna* e.g. the Āmahīyavasāman, in the second *stotriyā* (in the *ṛc* the word vari[3]vovi[1]t) - va[1]rivo[2ra1]vāit or, the beginning of *udgītha* which has low *svara* gets the high *svara* e.g. Auśanasāman (Ūha Daśa 4), the word *dra*[2ra]*va*[3] gets the high *svara* in the *parvan* — *dra*[1]*vā pari ko*[ra]*śām*.

(8) *nīca* - the syllable having the high *svara* in the *yoni* gets low *svara* in the *ūha* e.g. in the Samantāsāman (Ūha.Sam

2 1ra 2ra 1
224) the *parvan* apovasānoarṣasāi which begins the *udgītha* in the first *stotriyā*. In the *yoni* (G.G.G. 61-1) the
1 ra 2ra 1
first *parvan* of the *udgītha* is tvaṃhotānoadhvarāi which has high *svara*.

(9) *sandhivat* - even in the absence of proper reason, where *sandhi* is not expected it is made in the *gāna*, e.g. Śaṅkusāman (Ūha. Sam 250) in the second *stotriyā* the
[1]
parvan mado | *yasya*. . . . The *parvan madaḥ* is there and then *yasya* etc. occur. In the *padapātha* the word *madaḥ* ends in *visarga*. In the *gāna* also the word ought to have ended in *visarga*. But it is chanted as *mado*.

(10) *padavat* - when in the *ṛc* there is *sandhi* as per its rules, in the *gāna* such a *sandhi* is absent e.g. Bhāradvājasāman
1 2 – 1 2
(Ūha. Sūtra 711) - brahmāyūꞅ1- jāꞅ2ḥ | hārayai |

(11) *atva* - the vowel *ā* becomes *a* e.g. Vārāhasāman (Ūha.
2 3 4 5
Ahīna 651) - dhuḥpavākāḥ. In this *parvan* the vowel *ā* of the word *pāvakāḥ* has become *pavākāḥ*.

(12) *ārbhāva* - the *vṛddha* vowel *ṛ* becomes *ār* e.g.
[2] 1
Kārṣṇasāman (G.G.G. 491.1) the *parvan* ghnantāḥkā-
2
ꞅ23rṣṇāmū. (*kṛṣṇa* is changed into *kārṣṇa*)

(13) *praśleṣa* - the form arrived at in the *ṛc* is kept in the same state in the chant e.g. Saṁkṛtisāman (Ru 24), second
[2]ra 1 2ra
stotriyā-nunampu nā no vibhiḥ.

(14) *visleṣa* - the vowel *a* which has been merged in the preceding vowel is chanted separately e.g.
2ra 1 2ra 1ra 2
Devasthānasāman (RG23) nūnampunānoavibhāɾ3iḥ.

(15) *saṁkṛṣṭa* - the conjunct consonant is chanted in the same
2 1
form e.g. Kāvasāman (Ūha. Daśa 13) abhyovā.

(16) *vikṛṣta* - a vowel is inserted in the conjunct consonant e.g. *sūrya* is chanted as *sūriya*, in the Baṇmahānai--
[2]ra 2
pātithasāman (Ūha. Kṣu 935) - ... Sūriyāɾ3el

(17) *lopa* (elision) - e.g. in the Bārhadgirasāman (Ṛv 12) the
[2] 1
visarga is elided in the *parvan*..... nṛbhāi (the *visarga* of the word *nṛbhiḥ* is dropped). In the Gāyatrasāman, (at the beginning of the G.G.G.) the consonant *ṭ* is elided in the
1 2 1 1 1
ending dāyo | - āɾ345 | (The final word of the *ṛc* is *pracodayāt*).

(18) *atihṛti* - *anusvāra, sparśa* and *repha* when followed by *stobha* pass over it and are joined to the syllable of the *ṛc* [In the first *Parkasāman* (G.G.G. 1) there is the ending
1 3 5ra ra 3 5
tsāɾ2ibāɾ234 auhovā | hīɾ234ṣī. (The *repha* of *barhiṣī* is

elided. When there is pause at the end of the *stobha* these *anusvāra, repha* etc. are elided. In the case of *sandhi* there is no elision). In the Saubharasāman (G.G.G.
5 ra ra ra 4 5
109.3) in the *parvan* taṁgūrdhayāsvauhorṇārām, the *stobha* comes after *sva*, the *repha* in *svarṇaram* crossing the *stobha auho* is joined to the next syllable *ṇā*.

(19) *ābhāva* - the *vṛddha tālavya* coming in the midst of a word becomes *ā* when the *stobha* beginning with *ha* follows e.g. in the Saubharasāman (Ūha. Eka 388) -
na 2
nadāʃ3hāʃ3i (the word of the *ṛc* is na dīdhimaḥ).

(20) *vikalpa* - in the same foot, sometimes there is two-fold chant. In the performance one of the alternatives is to be employed, e.g. Rauravasāman (Ūha. Daśa 59) -
1ra ra 2 1ra ra 2
nemintaṣṭevasūʃ23hāi | nemintaṣṭe vasāʃ23uhāi.

(j) The Form of Sāman

The *svarūpa* form is the one which is employed in the sacrificial performance while the form used in the *svādhyāya* (daily recital) is the *rupāntara* one. The Ṛgvedic recitation employed three pitches high, middle and low. These were rendered as musical notes in the chants of Sāmaveda. The *mantras* are recited in one tone in the case of *japa* etc. The

Śatapathabrāhmaṇa is recited with two accents, high and low, when three tones, high, middle and low are used in the recitation, the efficacy of utterance was achieved in a greater measure. The *ṛcs* being metrical, the metrical rhythm provided impetus to the rendering of metres like Gāyatrī with musical notes. The Sāmaveda gives this musical rendering of the *ṛcs*. B. Faddegon opines that in the Ṛgveda high tones of Bhāṣā are lowered to the middle pitch, although they are called *udāttas*. Hence, the curved after tones rise above all the other syllables and the formerly *udātta* syllables are on the same pitch with the *pracaya* syllables. But in some cases the latter part of *svarita* was recited like *anudātta* or even lower. Dr. Sankaran says that the *pracayasvara* was the keynote in the four-notes stage of ancient *Sāman* music. The major changes that are effected in the form of the *ṛc* for the purpose of music and the magical effect of the chants are as follows:

(1) Vikāra (modification) e.g. a^{1}gne rendered as o^{4}gnāi;

(2) Viśleṣaṇa (disjunction) e.g. vī^{1}taye rendered as vo^{1}itayāʃ2i;

(3) Vikarṣaṇa - (protraction) e.g. ye^{1} is rendered as yā^{1}ʃ23yi;

(4) Abhyāsa - (repetition) e.g. to^{1}yāʃ2yi | to^{1}yāʃ2yi |

(5) Virāma - (pause) - used for the sake of gāna though not

the word-ending) - gṛṇāṇo havyadātaye is rendered with

1ra 2ra

a pause after *ha* of *havya*, gṛṇānoha I vyadātoyāɾ2i;

(6) Stobha - the additional syllables over and above those of the *ṛc*) e.g. - *hāi, hāu, vā, as* etc.

The musical form of the chant is effected by the employment of musical notes (*svaras*), the syllabic modifications (*puṣpa*) and the additions of the *stobha* syllables. The essence of *Sāman* is the *svara*.

The *Sāman* has five divisions called *bhaktis*. When Ōm is added before *prastāva* and *udgītha*, the *Sāman* becomes endowed with seven divisions. The parts of the *bhakti* are called *parvans*. The *Sāman* with the five divisions forms a *stotrīyā* of the *stotra*. These five divisions are - the *prastāva, udgītha, pratihāra, upadrava* and *nidhana*. In the sacrificial performances, there are three main Sāman-chanters - the *prastotṛ* chants the *prastāva*; the *udgātṛ*, the *udgītha*; the *pratihartṛ*, the *pratihāra*; the *upadrava* by the *udgatṛ* and the *nidhana* by all the three together. The *upagātṛs* numbering three to six chanted the *upagāna* with *ho* in the *pañcamasvara* (i.e. the *mandra*-note) in the *pluta* manner (i.e. protracted manner) and the sacrificer chanted *Om* in the *prathamasvara*.

This *upagāna* started from *himkāra* and continued till the *nidhana*, covering the intervals between the notes used in the divisions. It was stopped when the chanting of *nidhana* began.

All the divisions are to be sung without taking breath or the chanters may take breath in the midst of the foot or *stobha*. They are not to take breath in between two feet or two *stobhas*. In the Tāṇḍyabrāhmaṇa (7.1.8), the *aniruktagāna* of the Gāyatrasāman is given. The word *anirukta* is explained by Sāyaṇa as *avyaktākṣara* (i.e. having the syllable not clearly manifested). In the Bahiṣpavamāna of Agniṣṭoma, *Ōm* is substituted in place of the syllables of the *ṛc*. This *brāhmana* has also stated the *upagāna* of the wives in the Mahāvrata with specific *vīṇās* (see p.160 of the Chowkhamba edition, 5.6.8).

The *stotra* consists of *stotrīyās*. In the *stotra* the same *Sāman* is chanted in the case of the three *ṛcs* (*tṛca*). When in the *pragātha* which has two *ṛcs*, it is so arranged that the two *ṛcs* make three *stotrīyās*. The word *yoni* means the source verse of the *Sāman*. In the case of *tṛcagāna*, the first *stotrīyā* is also called *yoni*. There are some *stotrīyās* having one *ṛc*.

The *Sāmans* mentioned in the Sāmaveda are three-fold. The chanting of the *Sāman* based on the *stobhas* without any basis of the *ṛc* is called *channagāna* (i.e. the chant keeps its concealed nature), that having the *ṛc* and the *stobha* is termed as *leśa-gāna*; and the one consisting of the *ṛc* and having no *stobha* is called *āvirgāna*; (as it consists of the *ṛc* only the clarity of meaning becomes manifest). In the *leśagāna*, as the word suggests the clarity is partly mystified by the addition of the *stobhas*.

In the Vedasaṁhitas the *Sāmans* are mentioned with their *stomas*. *Stoma* means a group of *stotriyās*. Each *stotra* consists of a *sūkta* normally having three *ṛcs*. In some cases, the number of *ṛcs* is more also. The *stomas* are nine having the number of the *stotriyās* as 9, 15, 17, 21, 27, 33, 24, 44 and 48. The illustration of *pañcadaśastoma* is given below to have an idea. As the appellation indicates it has 15 *stotriyās* - In the first *paryāya*, (i.e. round), the first *ṛc* is chanted thrice and the second and third once each only. In the second round, the first *ṛc* is chanted once, the second *ṛc* chanted thrice, and the third *ṛc* once; in the third round, the first and the second *ṛcs* are chanted once each, and the third thrice. In this manner, the total number of fifteen is arrived at. This is the first *viṣṭuti*. The number fifteen is arrived at in the second *viṣṭuti* in a different manner. In the first round, the first *ṛc* is sung thrice and the second and the third once each. In the second round, all the three *ṛcs* are sung once each. In the third round, the first *ṛc* is sung once, the second thrice, and the third thrice. In the third *viṣṭuti*, in the first round, the first, second and the third *ṛcs* are chanted once each; in the second round the first *ṛc* is chanted once, the second thrice and the third once; in the third round, the first *ṛc* is chanted thrice, the second once and the third thrice. These are the three *viṣṭutis* of the *pañcadaśastoma*. The *viṣṭutis* thus formed by the distribution through the process of repetition of the *stotriyās* over the three rounds have special names, e.g. the third *viṣṭuti* of this *stoma* is called *udyati*. The particular stick used to measure the number of *stotriyas* is called *kuśā*. The *prastotṛ* places it on the piece of cloth called *kuśāstaraṇa*. A specimen of *kuśāvidhāna* for the *pañcadaśastoma* is as follows:

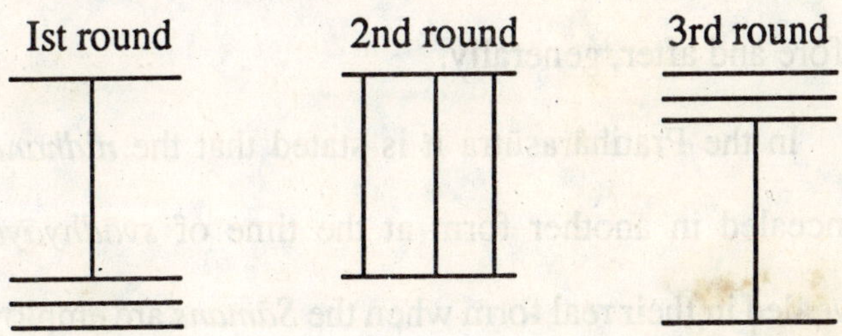

The total number of *viṣṭutis* in all the stomas comes to 28. They have special names. The particular *viṣṭuti* is to be employed for the fulfilment of the particular desire as per the prescription laid down by the sacrificial literature.

The *stobha*, following the *prastāva* is the part of it; the *stobha* preceding the *udgītha* is the part of *udgītha*. When there is the repetition of the part of a foot, the *prastāva* is formed by that foot along with the repeated portion. The *prastāva* is of two syllables, four syllables, of two feet etc. Some *Sāmans* are to be sung by the *prastotṛ* alone. They are called *Parisāmans*. There are two *pṛṣṭhas* in the Soma sacrifice. They are the Rathantara and the Bṛhat. The *stotras* are divided according to the *pṛṣṭhas*. Those *Sāmans* which have the syllables of the *ṛc* in the *nidhana* are *antarṇidhanas*. If the syllables other than those of the *ṛc*, are employed in the *nidhana*, the *Sāmans* are *bahirṇidhanas*. At the time of chanting the *stotras*, the *ṛcs*, that are the *yonis* are recited before and after, generally.

In the Pratihārasūtra it is stated that the *nidhanas* are concealed in another form at the time of *svādhyāya*, but revealed in their real form when the *Sāmans* are employed in rituals. They are called the *channanidhanas*. The *nidhanas* coming at the end of the *Sāmans* are *sāmāntika* ones, while those that are used in the midst of the *Sāman* are called *antaḥsāmīka* ones. The former are of four types - *svara, nidhana, iḍā* and *vā*. *Vā* is called *upāya* also. *Svaranidhana* is that when the final syllable of the *ṛc* has *svarita* accent and is turned into the svāra and hāi. This svāra has the form the *padānusvāra* or *parisvāra*; its form is 5_{656} i.e the numeral 5 is the primary svara and 656 are the secondary *svaras* coming in between the line. The word *padānusvāra* indicates nasalization. Nidhana is of two types - *padanidhana* and *bahirnidhana*. Adhyardheḍā is of the nature of *iṭ iḍā*.

(k) Nāradīyaśikṣā

Nāradīyaśikṣā mentions in detail the merits and demerits of chanting e.g. *rakta* (melodious), *sukūmāra* (having gentle words), *madhura* (having charming words) etc. are the merits which number ten. The demerits are like singing with fear or agitated mind, unclear, nasal, harsh, out of time, *pluta* uttered in quick manner, irregular employment of *vṛttis* etc. The proper manner of chanting stated in the Lāṭyāyanaśrautasūtra (9.10.18) is as follows : (1) *Agrasta* - no syllable should be omitted; (2) *avyasta* - it should be well connected; (3) *avilambita* - the utterance should not be too slow or too fast; (4) *anambūkṛta* - it should not be uttered while emitting saliva from the mouth; (5) *uraḥpratiṣṭhita* - the chanting ought to be done with the notes produced from the chest; (6) *adantāghātita* - the teeth must not strike against each other while the syllables of the chant are being uttered.

(l) The Names of the *Sāmans*

(1) based on the *chandas* e.g. Gāyatra is based on the Gāyatrī chandas; Bṛhat on the Bṛhatīchandas, Vairāja on the Virājchandas, Śākvara on the Śakvarīchandas etc.;

(2) based on the names of the sages who revealed the *Sāman* e.g. Saindhukṣita revealed by the sage Sindhukṣit, Āuśana revealed by Uśanas, Āmahīyava revealed by the sage Amahīyu, Nārmedha revealed by the sage Nṛmedhas etc.;

(3) based on the portion at the beginning of the *ṛc* or the portion that occurs afterwards, e.g. Viśoviśīya, Yajñāyajñīya etc.;

(4) based on the *nidhana* e.g. Dāvasunidhana, Okonidhana, Īnidhana etc.;

(5) based on the purpose e.g. Rākṣoghna, Ariṣṭa, Abhīvarta (employing this *Sāman* gods went to heaven - *abhyavartanta*), Divākīrtya (when Svarbhānu encompassed the sun by darkness, gods destroyed the darkness by employing the Divākirtyasāman) etc.;

(6) miscellaneous type - Vīṅka, Saṁvarga etc.

(m) The Results of Sāmans

In the Ṣaḍviṁśabrāhmaṇa the chanting of specific *Sāmans* is prescribed to remove the evil effects that would accrue by performing the particular rites. In the Sāmavidhānabrāhmaṇa, particular *Sāmans* are stated for the purpose of securing gold, destroying *bhūta, preta* (i.e. the ghosts, goblins) etc. The Ekavṛṣasāman is prescribed to make the coronated king, a sovereign emperor. Obtainment of heaven is the main result.

The *stobhas* are significant from the point of the result of the *Sāmans*. They are supposed to have mystic effects. The *stobha* is defined by Jaimini as *'adhikaṃca vivarnaṃ' ca.* Sāyaṇa states that when additions are to be made, the syllables that are employed different from those of the *ṛc* are called *stobha*. The *varṇa* in his explanation is to be understood as the group of syllables also by the maxim '*jātau ekavacanam*' (i.e. singular is understood to indicate class). They are of three types - (1) *varṇastobha* - ī, e etc. (2) *padastobha - atha, iha, iḍā* etc. (3) *vākyastobha* - e.g. *aganma jyotiḥ* | *amṛtā abhūma*; *namoऽnnāya* namoऽnapataye etc. There appears to be some meaning in the case of the *vākyastobhas*. The *stobhas* help the musicalness and contain the symbolic praise of the deities. The Akṣaratantra treats the *stobhas* in detail.

(n) The First Two Chapters of the Puṣpasūtra

In the first two chapters of the Puṣpasūtra, the *Samāns* of the Uttaragāna are given in the order of the *parvans* (chapters). The *parvan* is divided into *khaṇḍas* and each *khaṇḍa* is divided into several *sūtras*. The Pūrvagāna consists of the Gramegeya or Veyagāna and Araṇyegeyagāna. The Uttaragāna consists of the Ūha and the Ūhya or Rahasyagāna. The former is based on the Veyagāna and the latter mainly on the Āraṇyakagāna. The students learn the melodies of the Pūrvagāna. Their sacrificial employment is carried out as per the Ūha and the Ūhyagāna. There was no commentary available on the first two chapters in which the first part of the *sūtra* mentions the syllables or words at the beginning of the *yoni* i.e. the *ṛc* on which the *Sāman* is based. The second part constitutes a portion of the name of the *Sāman* in the *pratīka* form (i.e. symbolic manner). Fortunately, now, the manuscript copy of the commentary of Nānābhāi Dīkṣita is available in which he has stated the sacrificial employment along with certain details of these *Sāmans*. A few points from this commentary are mentioned below to understand the details of *viniyoga* of these *Sāmans*.

The first *sūtra* of the first *khaṇḍa* of chapter I, is given as *uccā mahī*. The *sūtra* is explained as follows : The Amahīyavasāman is based on the *tṛca* beginning with *uccā te*. Its sage is Amahīyu, Chandas Gāyatrī and deity Soma. It is employed in the Mādhyandina Pavamāna of the Jyotiṣṭoma. In the Soma sacrifice there are three *savanas* (pressing of the Soma plant) (to be offered to the deity). The *Prātaḥsavana* (morning libation), *Mādhyandinasavana* (mid-day offering) and the *Tṛtīyasavana* (evening offering). The Soma sacrifices described in the first five *parvans* are - Daśarātra (performed for ten days); Saṁvatsara (performed for one year); Ekāha (one day sacrifices); Ahīna (from two to eleven days) and Satra (to be performed by several sacrificers together). The

Prāyaścittaparvan states the *Sāmans* that are to be employed when such defects as the breaking of the jar, excess of the offering of *sōma* etc. happen, to remove these defects for the proper fulfilment of the sacrifice. In the last *Kṣudraparvan*, the *stotras* to be employed in the Soma sacrifices that are not stated in the present work but given in the Brāhmaṇas of Ṛgveda etc. or those having meagre results are given. There are some *Sāmans* which have two *pratihāras* one of which is to be employed e.g. the Kautsasāman (Ūha Daśa 30) has alternatively two *pratihāras*, consisting of four syllables. The Yauktāśvādyasāman (Ūha Daśa 39) is to be employed in the Mādhyandinapavamāna. In this *Sāman*, the preceding *stobha*
2ra 1 2 1 2
is to be chanted by the *pratihārtṛ* e.g. - auhohohāi | viśvā || In the Agnestriṇidhanasāman (Ūha Daśa 88) there is the
[3] 5
antarṇidhana e.g. - vīʃ234nām, in the first *stotriyā;* after the *pratihāra* of four syllables, there is another *antarnidhana*-
[3] 5
rāʃ234yā | (the *antarṇidhana* has the *svara* of the *nidhana*). The Vāmrasāman (Ūha Daśa 87) has two *pratihāras* - e.g.
1 - 1 -
(1st *stotriyā*) - māndrāʃ2yāyā2 || is the first one which is the regular one of four syllables and the other one is of two
1 -
syllables—rayā2 || .. It has the *adhyardheḍānidhana* i.e. in

place of *ūpā,* there is *iṭ iḍāʃ*32345. The Santanisāman (Ūha Dáśa 90) is employed in the Ārbhava, on the fifth day in the *dáśarātra* of the *dvādaśaha.* It has *prastāva* in the first *stotriyā* only. In the Pārthsāman (Ūha Dáśa 94), the *prastāva* preceded by stobha, the *udgitha,* the *pratihāra* and the *upadrava* are formed by the 1st, 2nd, 3rd and the 4th foot respectively. The Krauñcasāman (Ūha Daśa 100) has the *tṛca* in the Gāyatrīmetre. There is the repetition of the 2nd foot - e.g. - (1st *stotriyā*) -

1 2 1 2 na 2 3 5 1 na
pāvasvāmā | dhu ʃ 3ma | tā ʃ234 māḥ || and, pavasvamadhumā
3 5
ʃ 32 | tā ʃ 234māḥ ||. One of these two repetitions is to be employed. The Vāravantīyasāman (Ūha Ekāha 458) - It has the following *pratihāras* - (1) with seven syllables before the
2 1 5 1ra ra 2 3ra 4ra 5
stobha ihā — pavāitre ʃ 234 hāi | somoakṣā ʃ 34 | auhovā | (*pavitre somo akṣarat* |; (2) ending in foot beginning with
2 3 2 1 5
uhuvā - uhūvā ʃ 234 rāt; (3) the regular one i.e. pavāitreʃ234hāi
1ra ra 2 3ra 4ra 5 1 3 5 2 3
| somoakṣā ʃ 234 | auhovā | ihā ʃ 234 hāi | uhuvā ʃ 234 rāt ||; Āmahīyavasāman (Ūha Ekāha 408) is employed in the middle *stotrīyā* of the 1st Agniṣṭut (there are 4 Agniṣṭutsāmans) etc. The general rule is that the *stobha* preceding the *pratihāra,* forms part of the *udgītha* and is chanted by the *udgātṛ*; while that following the *pratihāra,* by *partihartṛ.* There are some

exceptions to this rule. The *Sāmans* are divided into two broad groups - *viṣamabhakti* and *vibhāgya*; in the former the feet are not evenly divided, while in the latter, they are equally divided in different *bhaktis*.

The *Vibhāgyasāmans* are of three kinds -

(i) *Padavibhāgya* - In them the feet of the verse are equally divided among the *bhaktis*, devoid of *stobha*; e.g. The Pravadbhāragavasāman (Ūha Daśa 127)

(ii) *Sastobhapadavibhāgya* - In these, the feet of the verse-chant, along with the *stobhas* form the different *bhaktis* - e.g. the Mahāvaiśvāmitrasāman (Ūha Daśa 98)

(iii) *Stobhavibhāgya* - In them, the *stobhas* like, *vā, hāi, ihā* etc. are divided among *bhaktis*, leaving the feet to form themselves as *nidhanas* e.g. *Aṅgirasāmgoṣṭhaḥ* (Ūha Daśa 106).

The *nidhanas* also are presented to secure the desired results. The *nidhanas* of particular *Sāmans* were to be chanted in a particular manner such as, in forceful voice, in hissing sound or in tinkling tone etc. The change of *nidhana* depended on the caste of performer also e.g. the original *nidhana* of Saṁśānasāmans was to be changed in the case of the Kṣatriya and the Vaiśya. The *nidhanas* were to be changed in the sacrifices performed to destroy one's enemies and those performed with good intentions. One desiring rain should have the *nidhana* '*hiṣī*' while employing the Saubharasāman. In the case of the four Saṁśānasāmans (G.G.G . 258.1), there are four *nidhanas* - '*saṁśravase,*' '*viśravase,*' '*satyaśravase*' and '*śravase.*' In regard to them, '*jityai*' should be employed in the place of '*śravase,*' in the case of the Kṣatriya sacrificer; and '*puṣṭyai*' in the case of the Vaiśya, according to some. It is as follows : '*saṁjityai,*' '*vijityai,*' '*satyajityai*' and '*jityai*'; '*sampuṣṭyai,*' '*vipuṣṭyai,*' '*satyapuṣṭyai*' and '*puṣṭyai.*' (Drāhyāyaṇaśrautasūtra 1306); etc. The *nidhana* would be a single syllable or a word or even a line of the verse itself.

(o) The Schools of Sāmaveda

It is stated that the Sāmaveda has thousand (*Sahasravartmā Sāmavedaḥ*) śākhas. This statement appears perhaps to be due to the convention indicating the large number of *Sāman* chants. The tradition available from the *purāṇas* etc. is as follows:

Vyāsa taught Sāmaveda to his pupil Jaimini. Jaimini

taught it to Sumantu, who in turn gave it to Sutvā. From Sutvā, Sukarmā obtained it. Sukarmā enlarged it into 1000 *saṁhitās*. Sukarmā had two sons - Pauṣpiñji and Hiraṇyanābha. Pauṣpiñji established 500 *saṁhitās* and Hiraṇyanābha 500 *saṁhitās*. The followers of the former are the northern *Sāmagas* and of the latter, the eastern *Sāmagas*. Pauṣpiñjī's pupil is Laugākṣī and his four pupils were Kuthumi and others. Kuthumī had three pupils. Such tradition is found in the case of Hiraṇyanābha also. Caraṇavyūha also says that the Sāmaveda has 1000 types. Those, the study of which was undertaken even during the period when the study was prohibited, were destroyed by Indra with his thunderbolt. In the Bauddha work, 'Divyāvadāna,' it is mentioned that the Sāmaveda has 1080 schools. Among the *Saman* chanters, offering of the libations of water is enjoined for thirteen teachers.

PART II - PRESENT PRACTICE

(a) At present the three schools available are the Kauthuma, the Rāṇāyanīya and the Jaiminīya. Caraṇavyūha states that the Kauthumi is currently known prominently in Gujarat, Jaimini in Karṇātaka and Raṇāyanīya in Maharashtra. Caland opines that Tāṇḍya is another sub-school of Kauthuma. Srī Śaṅkarācārya points out that the Tāṇḍya and the Śāṭyāyana are two independent schools.

Among the *Sāman* chanters available now-a-days, the Kauthumas are more extensively found. The *Sāmagas* of this school are available in the South in Tamilnadu and Mysore states and in the North, in Gujarat and Bengal mainly. The Kauthumas of South are again divided into two styles - *prācīna* and *navīna pāṭha*. The Rāṇāyanīya followers are found among the Havik Brahmins of Karwar region. In Andhra region also there are two traditions of this school namely, Tāmraparṇīpāṭha and Gurjarapāṭha. The Kauthumas and the Rāṇāyanīyas have no difference as regards text. The Jaiminīya-school is found in Tamilnadu and Kerala. The Tamilnadu tradition is available at Śrīraṅgam in Tamilnadu and at Kaḍuntarapuḷḷi in Kerala near Palghat. The Nambudirī Jaiminīya tradition is found mainly in Pāñyal village. This tradition is completely oral at least up to the present day. A list of *Sāmans* recorded for the purpose of study is given in Appendix A.

A few *Sāmans* of each tradition are rendered by me with

the modern Hindustani notation of *Sargam.* This is done to bring out the difference between the modern rendering and the rendering indicated by the numeral notation as per the statement in the Nāradīyaśikṣā. The *Sāman* notes Prathama, Dvitīya etc. upto Saptama are identified in this Śikṣā with the notes of flute namely, Ma, Ga, Ri, Sa, Dha, Ni and Pa respectively. In the present practice, the reversal of the order stated in this Śikṣā is not found. The regular descending order Ni, Dha is seen. In the *Sāman* chants there was possibly no such distinction in the notes like the flat (*Komala*) and the sharp (*Tīvṛa*) variety of a note. The modern notation rendered in the *Sāmans* given below only indicates the notes approximately. In the absence of any Svara instrument, for accompaniment, the indications of notes by the Gātra-vīṇā alone, is bound to be approximate. As regards the duration of notes like short (*Laghu*), long (*Guru*) and protracted (*Pluta* or *Vṛddha*) as stated in the Mātrālakṣaṇa, it is observed that the Mātrālakṣaṇa statement does not fully hold good in the present practice. The correct nature of *Kruṣṭa* is not found out satisfactorily in the chanting of the expert *Sāman*-singers belonging to any available school. The *Sāman* chanting with all the above mentioned limitations has got to be understood. The importance of the present practice lies in the fact that the tradition of each school has been kept alive for centuries by the *Sāman* chanters.

Dr. Walter Kaufmann, in his article "Some Reflections on the Notations of Vedic Chant" has pointed out that the *kuśā* sticks used in the chanting of *Sāman* to count the number in regard to viṣṭutis, reminds us of the notation of the 'Shomyo,' the Buddhistic chant of Japan. He says that the use of fifteen wooden sticks was taken over by the Indian Buddhists from the Sāmavedins. After the notations of a few chants of the available chanting by expert chanters, I have added some information about the 'Shomyo' from the cassettes sent to me, just for the purpose of comparative study.

In regard to the applications of *Sāmans*, in the various rituals of the different Soma-sarifices, Ārṣeyakalpa becomes very helpful. While stating the lists of *Sāmans*, their basic *ṛcs* are mentioned in the symbolic form (*pratīka*). Arṣeyakalpa deals with Gavāmayana, Ekāhas, Ahīnas, Satras and Ayanas; the Kṣudrasūtra covers the sacrifices in the Prāyaścittaparvan and the Kṣudraparvan of the Ūhagāna.

Some Sāmans with Modern Hindustani Notations

गोतमस्य पर्कः (GGG. 1.1)

१ ४ २२ २ १

ॐ ओ ग्ना इ ॥ आ या ही ऽ३ वो इ तो या ऽर् इ।

सा ० ०॥ ग ग ग रे म ० म म ऽग

१ १ २ २२

तो या ऽरॆइ । गृ णा नो ह ।

म म ऽग । म म ग ग।

१ १

व्य दा तो या ऽरॆइ । तो या ऽरॆ इ ॥

ग म म म ग । म मऽग ॥

१ २२ १ १ ३

ना इ हो ता० सा ऽ२३ ॥ त्सा ऽ२ इ बा ऽ२३४

म ० ग म मऽग रे ॥ म ऽ ग ग रे ऽ ग रे सा

५२ २ ३ ५

औ हो वा ॥ ही ऽ२३४ षी ॥

ध ध ध रेऽगरेसाध ॥

कौ० द० सा नि धं सा॥ रे सा रेग्रेसा सा रे ग्रे रे ग् रे रेग् रेग् रेरे।

तिरुपति रे रेग्रे ग्रेरे् रे । रे रेग्रेग् रेसा सा ।

नवीन सा रेग्रेग् रेग्रेग् रे सा । रे ग्रे रेग्रेग् रे रे् सा ॥

पद्धति रे रे रेग्रेसा रेग्रेग् रेग् रे सा॥ रे ग्रे सा सा सानि्ंसा सानिधं

नि्ं रेसानि्धं नि्ंध ॥ नि्ं सा नि्ंधं नि्ंधं ॥

कौ० द० सा सा सा ॥ सा रे रे सा सा निं्सा सासा रे रे सा ।

म्हेसूर रे ग रे सा । रे ग ग रे सा ।

रे ग रेग रे सा । रे ग रे ग रे सा ॥ रे ग रे सा

रे ग रे ग रे सारेगरे सा ॥ रेग रेसा निं सा निं सा निं

निंसा नींधं नीधं ॥ रे निंसा निंघ निंघ ॥

कौ० उ० रथन्तरं साम - (R.G. Daśa. 1.) (तृचगानम्)

१ २ र र र

गुजरात ॐ ॥ आ भि त्वा शू र नो नु मी वा ॥

रर र र र

आ दु ग्धा इव धेनव ई शान मस्य ज ग तः ।

१ २ १ र २ १ ४

सु वा ऽ२३ई शाम् ॥ आ इ शा न मा ऽ२३ इन्द्रा ऽ३ ॥

१ र र ५ ५

सु स्थू ऽ२३४ षा । ओ वा ऽ६ । हा उ वा ॥ श्रीः ॥

रर १ २ र रर र

ई शो वा ॥ ना मिन्द्र सुस्थुषोन त्वावा ँ अन्यो दि विराः ।

१ २ १ ररर१ ४ १ र

न पाऽ२३र्यिवाः ॥ न जातोना ऽ२३ जाऽ३ ॥ नाइष्याऽ२३४ता ।

र ५ ५

ओ वा ऽ६ हा उ वा ॥ श्रीः ॥

२ २ र र र

न जी वा ॥ तोन जनिष्यते अश्वायन्तो मघवन्नि ।

१ र १ २ १ ४

द्रवाऽ२३जिनाः ॥ गव्यनास्त्वा ऽ२३ हाऽ३ ॥

१ र र ५ ५ १

वा मा ऽ२३४ हा । ओ वाऽ६ । हा उवा ॥ अस् ॥

Chanted by Ṛṣiśaṅkara Tripāṭhi

आ भि त्वा शू र नो नु मो वा ॥

सारे् रे् सारे् रे् सा सा रेसा निं् सारे् रे् सा ॥

आ टु ग्धा इ व धे न व ई शा न म स्य ज ग तः ।

सारे् रे् रे् रे् ग्रे् रे् रे् रे् रे् रे् रे् रे् रे् रे् रे् रे् ।

सु वा ऽ२३ ई शा म् ।।

सा सा निं् धं सा सा सा सा ॥ आ इ शा न मा ऽ२३

सारे् रे् सा रे्सानिं सारे् सासा नि्

न्द्रा ऽ३ ॥

सा रे् सा निं् ॥ सु स्थूऽ२३४ षा । ओ वा ऽ६

रे रे्सा रे्सा निं् सा रे् सा निं् । रे् सा रे् सा निं् ।

हा उ वा

रे्रे् रे् सां ॥ श्रीः ॥

ई शो वा ॥ ना मि न्द्र सु स्थु षो न

रे् रे् सारे्सा ॥ सारे् सारे् सानिं् सा रे् रे् निं्
(ग) (ग)
त्वा वा म् अ न्यो दि वि यः । न पाऽ३र्थि वाः ॥

रे् रे् ग्रे् ग्रे् रे् रे् रे् रे् । रे् सा रे्सानिं् सा॥

न जा तो नाऽ२३ जाऽ३ ॥ ना इ ष्या ऽ२३ ता ।

रे् सा सा रे् सा निं् सा रे्सानिं् । रे् रे् रे् सा नि् रे सानि ।

ओ वाऽ६ । हा उ वा

रे् रे् सा निं् । सा रे् सा रे्सानि् ॥ श्रीः ॥

न जो वा ॥ तो न ज निष्यते अ श्वा यन्तो

ग् ग्सा साग् सा ॥ ग् ग् सा सा सा सा ग् निं् निं् सा सा सा

म घ व न्नि । द्र वाऽ२३जि नाः ॥ ग व्य न्त स्त्वा ऽ२३हाँऽ३ ।

सा सा ग्सा सानिं्सा सा सा ग् निं् सा ग् सा ॥ निं् सा सा

ग्साग्निं् निधं ।

वा माऽ२३४ हा । ओवाऽ६ । हाउवा । अस्

निं् ग् सा ग् साग् साग् सा निं् । निं् निं् सा ग्सा । सा सा

साग्सा निं्गसा । रे् रे्सानिं् ॥

यज्ञायज्ञीयम (Ūha Daśa.14)

४ ३ ४ २ ४ ५
य ज्ञा ऽ ५ य । ज्ञा ऽ३ वो ऽ३ ग्ना या इ ॥

१ र २ १ २ २
गा इ रा गि रा । चा ऽ३ दा क्षा ऽ३ साइ ॥

१ १ र २
प्री ऽ२ म्व य म मृ त म् । जा ता ऽ२३ वा ।

१ २ १
हु म्मा इ। दा ऽ३२ साम् ॥ प्रा यं मित्र्

३ २
सु शा ऽ२ सि षा उ॥ श्रीः॥

१ २ १ २ १ २
प्रा याम्।। मा इ त्रा म् । सू ऽ३ शा सी ऽ३

२ र १र १
षाम्॥ ऊ र्जो न पाऽरे त स हि।

र २ १ २
ना या ऽ२३ मा हु म्माइ॥ स्मा ऽ३२ यूः॥

१ र ३ २
दा शे म हव्य दाऽ२ त या उ॥ श्रीः॥

१ २ १ २ १ २ २
दा शे ॥ मा हा। व्याऽ३ दा ता ऽ३ या इ।

१ र १ र २ १
भुवद्वाजे ऽ२ ष्व वि। ता भूऽ२३ वात्। हुम्माइ॥

२ १ र र ३ १११
वाऽ३२ र्ध्दाइ। ऊतत्राता तनू ऽ२ ना ऽ२ ७ वा ऽ३४५॥

K. Anakavur old style chanted by Pt. Ekambaraśāstri of Madras (The chanting has nasal quality and *Kampa*.)

य ज्ञा ऽ ५ य । ज्ञा ऽ ३ वोऽ३ग्ना या इ॥

धं सा धंसा धंसा धं। सा धंसा धंसा सा सा धं धं धं सा ॥

गा इ रा गि रा ऽऽ। चा ऽ३ दा ऽऽ क्षा ऽ३

सा रे सा सा सा ग सा रे रेसा । सा सा धं सा रे रे सा धं सा

सा इ । प प्रा ऽरे व य म मृ त म् ।

रे सा। रे सा रेरेसाधंसा धं सा रे सा रेसा सा सा।

जा ता ऽ२३ वा। हि म्मा इ

ग् ग् सा सा रेरेरे सारे सा। ग्सा सा रेरेरे साऽसा॥

दा ऽ३२ सा म्॥ प्रा ऽ ऽ य म् म्मि त्रम्

(माइ)

सा रेरेसाधंसा सा सा॥ रेसारेसा रे सारे रेसा

सू शा ऽ २ँ सि षा उ ॥ श्रीः॥

सा सा साग्सा रेरेरेसाधं धं सा सा॥

प्रा या म्॥ मा इ त्रा म्।

रे रेसा रेरेसा सा। रेरेसा रे सा रेरेरे सा।

२

सू ऽ३ शाँ सी ऽ३ षा म्॥

ग्सा ग्सा रेरेसा सा रेरे सा सा॥

ऊ र्जो न पा ऽर॒ तँ स हि

रे घं सा सारेरेसा सा ऽ सा रे सारेसा

ना या ऽ२३ मा।

रेरेसा सारेरे सा। हु म्मा इ।

ग्ऽसा रेरेरेसा सा

स्माऽ३२ यूः ॥ दा शे म ह

सा रेरेरे सासाऽसा ॥ रे सा रेरेरे साग् सा धं ग्

व्य ऽ२ दा त या उ ॥ श्रीः ॥

सा ऽ सा धं सा सा ॥ श्रीः ॥

दा ऽ शे ॥ मा ऽ हा डव्य ऽ३ दा

सा रेरेरे धंसा सा रेरेसाधंसा साधंसा रेसासा

ता ऽ३ या इ। मुव द्वा जे ऽ२ ष्व वि।

साधंसा सरेसा सा । धं ग् ग्सा ग्सारेरेसा धं सा ग् सा।

ता ऽ ऽ ऽ भू ऽ२३ वा त्। हु म्मा इ।

ग्सारेरेसा सारेसाधंसा सा सा। ग् साग् सा।

वा ऽ३२ र्ध्दा इ । ऊ त त्रा ता

साधंसा गंसा रे सा सा । सा रेरेसा ग् सा ग्सा ग् सा

त नू ऽ२ ना॑ऽ२ उ।। वा ऽ३४५।।

सा सा ग्सा धंसा सा ऽ सा ॥ साधं साधं साधं साधं सा सा॥

Kauthuma South
old style
Tanjore style
Putukode tradition — Chanted by Pt. Gopal Vadyar
(Pudukode) — (The chanting has nasal quality)

ओ ग्ना इ ॥ आ या हीऽ३ वो इ तो या ऽ२इ। तो या ऽ२ इ।

सा धं सा ।। सा ग्रेग्रे सारे ग्रे रे गरे ग्रे सा। ग्रे ग्रे ग्रे सा।
(touch to पं)

गृ णा नो ह। व्य दा तो याऽ२ इ। तो याऽ२ इ।।

सा ग्रेग्रे ग्रेगरे सा। सा ग्रे ग्रे ग्रेगरे सा। ग्रे गरे ग्रेसा सा।।

ना इ हो ता सा ऽ२३। त्सा इ बा ऽ२३४

ग्रे गरे ग्रे गरे रे ग्रे रे। ग् रे ग्रे सा सा सा धं

औ हो वा।। ही ऽ२३४ षी।

धं ग्रे धं सा सा धंऽ सा।।

Chanted by Pt. Narayana Vadhyar of Manjupur—

ओ ग्ना इ।। आ या ही वो इ तो या ऽ२ इ।

सा धं सा।। सा ग्रे गरे सा ग्रे रे ग्रे गरे ग्रे सा।

तो या इ। गृ णा नो ह।

सा ग्रेरेग्रे सा। सा ग्रे गरे ग्रे सा सा।

व्य दा तो या इ। तो याऽ२ इ

सा ग्रे गरे ग्रे (गरेग्रे) ग्रे रे रेग्रे सा

ना इ हो ता सा ऽ२३। त्सा इबा ऽ२३४

ग्रे रे ग्रे रे ग्रे रे रेग्रे सा रेग्रेरेग्रेरे से धं

औ हो वा। ही ऽ२३४ षी।।
(stress)

धं ग्रे सा। सा धं साधं सा।।

राणायनीय GGG 1.1-3)

कारवार Chanted by Pt. Vishveshvarbhatta of

हविक् राणायनीय Hosakole.

गोतमस्य पर्कः (GGG 1.7)

(१) सा धं सा ॥ रे ऽऽ रे ऽऽ ग्सा रे रे ग्रे सा सा।

रे रे सा सा। सा ग्रे ग्रे ऽऽसासा। सा ग्रे रे रे ग्रे

सासा रे ग्रे सा सा॥ रे सा ग्रे सारे रे रे ऽसासा॥

रे ऽ सासा निंसारेसानिं निं ग्रे धं सा॥ धं सा ऽऽ धं सा॥

(२) कश्यपस्य बार्हिव्यम् (GGG 1.2)

धंपंसा धंपं धं सा।। सा रे ऽऽ सासा। धं रेसा रे सा रे

सा ग् सा सा निं सा निं सा॥ धं सा ग्सा ग् सा निं निं रेऽसा

सा सा॥ सा सारे ग् रे सासा धं सासा धं । धरि साधंसा॥

धं सासासारे ऽ धं सा॥

The text of this chant

४५ ४र५र४ १ रर र २
अग्न आयाहिवी ॥ तयाइ। गृणानोहव्यदाता ऽ२३ याइ॥

१ र र २१ २ १ ३
नि हो ता सत्सिबर्हा ऽ२३ इषी। बर्हा ऽरॅ इषा ऽ२३४

५र रर २ १ १११
औ होवा॥ बर्हीऽ३ षी २३४५॥

Text of पर्क (GGG 1.3)

४ ५ ४र ५र ४ ४
अ ग्न आ या हि । वा ऽ५ इ त या इ॥

१र र २ २ २ २ ३ ५
गृणानो हव्यदा ऽ१ ता ऽ३ यै ॥ नि हो ताऽ२३४ सा॥

१ २ १ ५ ५
त्साऽ२३इबाऽ३। हा ऽ२३४ इ षो ऽ६ हा इ॥

धं पं सा सा धं सा। सा धं ऽऽ पं पं साधं सा॥

धं रेसा रेसा रे रे सारेसा ऽ सा सा॥ सा सा निं सा रे रे सा॥

रे ऽऽ सा सा रे ऽ। रे ऽऽऽ सा धं सा धंसा॥

5 5
[In this chant, in the *nidhana*, *ṣo*ऽ*6hāi* is the illustration of *Padānusvāra* which involves nasalization.]

Rāṇāyaṇīya–chanted by Late Pt. Lakṣmaṇaśāstrī Dravida of Poona (Recorded in the Deccan College)

गायत्रम् (chant before the beginning of GGG)

(as given in the text)

१ १ र
ओ म् ऽ३। त त्स वि तु र्व रे णि योम्।

१र र र १र र २
भार्गो दे व स्य धी मा ही ऽरे । धि यो योनः प्रचो ऽ१२१२।

१ १ २ १११
हिम् स्थि आ ऽरे । दा यो। आ ऽ३४५ ॥

सा निं रेरे। मरे रेमरे रे मरे रे पपमग्रे ग्रे ग्रे रे।

ग्रे पपमग्रे पमग्रे ग्रे ग्रे ग्रे ग्रे ग्रेग्रे सा। सा ममम ग्रे ममग्रे ग्रे ग्रे

सासा रे ग्रेग् सारे ग् रेसा। मरे रे ग्रे ग्रेसा। मरे मरे ग्रे ग्रे

सा निं धं निं पं सा नि् रेरे गरे सा नि् सा नि् धं निंप

सा नि् रेरे ॥ (This is the rendering in the modern notation) The chanter has given the text in his article published in Poona Orientalist (Vol. IV, pp.1-21) as follows, with the modern Hindustani notation

२ १ १ र १
ओ ऽ३ म्। त त्स वि तुर्वरेणि यो ऽ म्।

सा ऽ नी रे। रे रे रेरेरे र रेऽरे। ।

१र
भार्गो दे व स्य धीमाही ऽ२ ॥ धि यो यो नः

रे ऽ रे ऽ रे ऽ रे रे रेऽ रेऽ रेऽ सा ऽ॥ सा रेऽ रेऽ रे

२ऽ १११ १
प्र चो १२१२॥ हिम् आरे ॥ दा यो॥

रे सा ऽ रेऽसाऽरेसाऽ ।। रेरेरेऽ साऽ।। रेऽ रेऽ।।

२ १११
आ ऽ ३४५॥

सा ऽ नी ऽ ध ऽ प ऽ ॥

The chanter follows the sūtra-"प्रत्येकं षड्जभावेन।"

So he understands the starting note as *Sa.*

आज्यदोहसामन् (The 1st quarter of the 1st *ṛc* of the tṛca)

रर १र २ १ २ ३४५
मू र्धा नं दा इ॥ वा ऽ३ अ र॥ तिं पृथिव्याः ॥
रर रर रर रर ३ ४२५
हा उ हा उ हा उ। आ ज्य दोह म्। (thrice)

सा ऽ सा ऽ सा ऽ सा ऽ नी ध ऽ प (thrice)

साऽरे ऽ रे रेरे। सा ऽ नी रे रे ॥ सा नी ध प।

महावामदेव्य सामन् (Ūha Daśa-5 1st stotriyā)

३ र ४ २ ४र ५ १
का ऽ५या ॥ न श्चा ऽ३ इत्रा ऽ आ भू वात्॥ ऊ॥
र २ १र २ १ १ २ र २
ती स दा वृधः सा॥ रवा ॥ औ ऽ३ हो हा इ।
१ २ ३ र २ १
क या ऽ२३ श चा ई॥ ष्ठ यौ हो ऽ३। हि म्मा ऽ२॥
१ २
वा ऽ२ र्तो ऽ ३५ हा इ॥ श्रीः ॥ (As written in the MS

with the chanter)

३ र ४ २ ४र ५ १
का ऽ५या ॥ न श्चा ऽ३ इत्रा ऽ३ आ भू वात् ॥ ऊ॥

सा ऽ ध ध ऽ।। ध नी ऽ सा ऽ रे ऽसा नी ऽ नी ध ऽ ध

॥ ग॥

र २ १र २ १ १ २ र
ती स दा वृ ध : सा॥ रवा॥ औ ऽ३ हो हा इ

गऽ रे गऽ ग रे गऽ । गऽ ।। रे रेऽ सा साऽ रे रे।। इ०

Āndhra Guntur Tradition — Chanted by Prof. Lakṣmīnārāyaṇa of Hyderabad

प्रवद्भार्गवम्~ (GGG 557.3) [Madras Ed.]

२र १र २ १
प्रो अ या सा इ त् इ न्दु रि न्द्रा।

सागसा निं सा ग् सा साग्सा ग्सा। पं निं सा साग् सा।

१ र १
स्या ऽ२ नि ष्कृ ता म्॥ स रवा स ख्यूः।

सा ग्सा सा निं निं साग्सा सा ॥ निं सानिंसा सा ग्सा॥

२ १ १
न प्र मि ना। ता ऽ२ इ स ङ्कि रा म्॥

निं सा सा ग्साग्सा ग्सा ग्सानिं सा सा ग् सासा।

२ १ २ १
म र्य इ वा। यु व ति भा इः।

निं सा सा ग्सा। निं निं निं सा ग्सा सा।

१ २र १
सा ऽ२ म र्ष ता इ॥ सो मः क ला।

ग्सा ग्सानिं सा ग्सा ग्सा सा॥ ग्सा ग्सानिं निं सा ग्सा।

२र १ १र २
श्रे श त या। मा ऽ२ ना प था ऽ ३ १ उ॥

ग्सानिं पं निं साग्सा। ग्सा ग्सानिं ग्सा ग् निं ऽऽ साग्सा ग्सा॥

१ १ १
वा ऽ २ ३ ४ ५ ॥

ग्सा ग्सा निं निं साधं॥

श्यैतम् (GGG.235.3) (Rendered as per recording in Hindustani notation)

४ ३ ४ ५ र ३ २ ३र ४र ५
अ भि प्र व स्सु रा । ध सा ऽ३४ औ हो वा॥

सासा सा सा धं सा रे। रेधं धं सासा सा ग्रे सासा॥

१ २ १ ब
आ इ न्द्र मर्च। य था वि दाऽ२३४ इ॥

रे ग्रे रे ग्रे ग्सा सा। सा रे रे ग्रे धं धं सा सा॥

५ ५ १र २ १ २ १ २
ओ ऽ ६ हा। यौं ज रि तृ भ्यः। मा घा ऽ २ ३ वा।

रे ऽ ऽ । ग्रे सा सा रे सा। रे ग्रे रे सा सा।

१ ३ ५ २ १ र २ २
पु रू ऽ २̂। वा ऽ २ ३ ४ सूः ॥ स ह स्रे णा इ वा ऽ३शा॥

ग रे ग्रे। सा धं सा ॥ सा सा ग्रे ग्रेरेरेरे सा सा॥

१ २ १ ३ ५र र
हि म्मा येंऽ३। क्षाऽ२̂ ता ऽ २ ३ ४ औ हो वा।

मरे मरे रे । धं ऽ धं सा सा सा मरे सा सा॥

३ ५
वा ऽ२३४ सू॥

धं ऽ सा॥

[In the Guntur style, the higher note is touched slightly often, just as one touches the fire very quickly.]

जैमिनीय
तामिळनाडु परम्परा
कोडुंतरपुल्की

Chanted by Pt. Sahasrarāma Aiyar and others.

(GGG. 1-3).

(१) गौतमस्य पर्कः (२) कश्यपस्यबर्हिषीयम् (३) गौतमस्य चैव पर्कः

त त श घाच चा श टा श
(१) ओ ग्ना इ । आ या हि वा इ । ता या इ

सा रेसा रे सा । सा धंनिं रे सा सा रेसा । नि सा सा रेसा

टा श चा श चि
ता या इ। गृ णा नो ह व्या दा।

निंसा सा रेसा। सा ग् ग् सानिं रेसा रेसा।

टा श टा श कि च
ता या इ ता या इ। ना इ हो ता।

सा सा रेसा सा सा रेसा। निं सा सा रेसा।

ट ट स शि ख मं
सा त्सा इ बा औ हो वा। ही ऽऽऽ षी॥

सा रेसा निं सानिं निं रेसा रेसा। सारेसारेसारेसा निंसा॥

तू षी
(२) अ ग्न आ या हि वी। त या इ गृ णानो

मिं रेसा सा रेसा निं रेसा। पं निं निं निं निं निं

ट त श चा शि टा ता
ह व्य दा तो या इ। नि हो ता स त्सी ब र्हा इषी।

निं सा रेसा रेसासानिं रेसा रेसा। सा ग् ग् ग् ग् निं रेसा रे सा।

टा ता
बा र्हा इ षा

निं रेसा निं सा सा ऽ ऽ निं।

शि चटास
औ हो वा।   ब हीं षी।।

निं रेसा निं।   सा रेसा निं।।

तू विश
(३) अ ग्न आ या हि वा इ त या इ।

पं निं निं निं निं रेसा सा निं रेसा निं।

पूय प श
गृ णा नो ह व्य दा ता ये नि हो

पं निं निं निं सा रेसा निं सारेसानिंनिं पं निं

रिव ण ट वा प
ता सा त्। सा इ बा र्हा ऽऽ

निं सा निं । रेसा रेसा निं सा रेसा रेसा निं धं

श शा
इ षो हा इ।।

धं निं निं रेसा।।

The *svara* is denoted by the syllable over the letter of the text. *ka* denotes the *svara* for one letter, *kā* for two, *ki* for three, *kī* for 4, *ku* for five and *kū* for six letters. In this way the *svara* should be understood in the case of the syllables over the textual letters.

Tū (*ta* denoting *āvartasvara*) stands for all the six letters combined; *Tī* for four letters combined) etc. After writing the *svaras* over the letters as per the text, I have rendered the chants in the modern Hindustani notation, just below the letters of the text. The syllable *śa* indicates the absence of *svara* and it always comes after the *svara* symbols. Ṣa also denotes the same, but it comes before the *svara*-symbol.

Nambudirī Jaiminīya — Chants (GGG. 1-3) sung by Toṭṭam Subrahmaṇyam Nambudiripāda.

(GGG. 1-3) [The notation is made by Dr. Sudha Patwardhan.]

(१) ओ ग्ना इ। आ या हि वाइ । ता या इ

सा ऽ ऽ सा ऽऽ गासा। निं ऽऽऽ गसा निं सा सा। साऽऽ सा सा

ता या इ । गृ णा नो ऽऽऽ ह व्या दा । ता या इ

गसा सा सा। धं सा सा ऽऽऽ धं सा सा धं सा सा सा

(ता या इ।) ना इ हो ता। सा त्सा इ बा औ हो वा।

(धं सा सा सा) सा सा सा सा। सा सा सा सा निं ग्सा सा।

ही षी॥

सा ग् ग् सा सा॥ (see at the end of Appendix A)

(२) अ ग्तऽ आ या हि वी। त या, इ गृ णा नो

निं सा ऽ सा ऽऽ सा ऽऽ सा ऽ सा। सा ग्रे रे सा ग्रे रे

हऽव्य दा ता या इ। नि हो ता स त्सि

ग्रेरे सा ऽ सा सा ऽऽ सा । निं सा सा सा सा

ब र्हा इ षी। बा र्हा इ षाँ ऽऽऽ औ हो वा।

सा सा सा सा। निं सा सा सा ऽऽऽ धं रेसा सा।

ब र्हीं षी॥

सा रे रेसा॥

(३) अग्न आऽऽया हि वा इ त या इ।

धं सा साऽऽ सा सा सा सा सा सा सा।

गृ णाऽ नो ह व्य दा ता ये।

धं सारे सा सा सा सा सा सा।

नि हो ताऽ सा ऽऽ त्। सा इ बा र्हा

निं सा रेऽ सा रेरे सा। सारेरे सा सा रे

इ षो हा इ॥

निं सा रेसा सा॥

The Jaiminīya style of Nambudirīs is marked by the prominence of *kampa* (shake) in it. The main note seen in this rendering is *sā*. Occasionally *Dha, Ni, Re* and *Ga* occur but in a very small measure. The main note *Sa* in this style is the basic one. The *kampa* dominates so much that the chanter prolongs it to the extent of being short of breath, often. It is difficult to notate it.

(b) The following is the information of the Shomyo (*Stotra* of Buddha) of the Soto sect of Zen Buddhism in Japan. The monks worship the image of Buddha. After this, the leader will sit down and start the *stotra*. Before the starting of *stotra*, gong will be sounded. The drums made of wood are played at the time of recitation. The hall will be purified with water by the leader. While the hall is being purified, the monks will recite another *stotra*. The purificatory water is sprinkled by sticks by the leader. All the acts of worship are performed by the leader, while the monks recite. While reciting, the monks move in a circle. After the purification ceremony the monks will recite the praise of Buddha. The beginning of the *stotra* is started by the monk who is good at recitation and then the other monks follow. There are salutations with the names of Buddha.

The notes employed are five corresponding to Sa, Ga, Ma, Pa, Dha. The music has five tones. The note Ni is also heard. The starting pitch is changed by one note higher in the course of recitation. Ma is chanted employing the ascent from Ga by the *mīṇḍa*.

(c) There is no clear cut distinction like the flat and sharp varieties of notes observed in the present *Sāman* chanting. However, effort is made to point out whether the note is *komala* (flat) by sign, ˎ e.g. नि॒ and whether it is in the lower register by writing the sign '.' over the note e.g. निं. Musically notes are approximations as the chanters depend only on *gātravīṇā* indications. There is no accompaniment of any *svara*-instrument as a rule. There are some variations in the chanting of different traditions. The notes Ga, Re, Sā, Ni, Dha, Pa are found forming the *Sāman* scale. Ma is rarely seen.

The *Sāman* scale	Numeral Indications
Kruṣṭa	11
Prathama	1
Dvitīya	2
Tṛtīya	3
Caturtha	4
Mandra	5
Atisvārya	6

Corresponding modern Hindustāni notes 1=Ma; 2=Ga; 3=Re; 4=Sa; 5=Ni; 6=Dha. Pa is the Lowest note (taken as *kṛṣṭa* note) in the chanting of the present chanters.

Corresponding Western Notation

Ma	F
Ga	E
Re	D
Sa	C
Ni	B
Dha	A
Pa	G

While giving the modern notation of the *Sāman* chanting, I have taken help of the two expert vocalists of Pune namely, Dr. Sudha Patwardhan and Prof. Shashikala Shirgopikar. As the notes employed by the chanter are not musically exact, it is possible that there would be some difference in regard to the identification of the notes employed in the chanting. My efforts are meant only to give some idea of the *Sāman* chanting available at present.

Appendix A

The list of recordings made by me and also those available from other sources is given here.

Living Traditions of Sāman chanting

(A) (1) Kauthuma (South)

(I) Chanted by Pt. Ekāmbara Dīkṣita in the Śrīveṅkaṭeśvara Pāṭhaśālā, Tirupati

(i) Yajñāyajñīyam (Ūha. Daśa. 14)

(ii) Rathantaram (RG. Daśa. 1)

(iii) Ājyadohāni (AG. 25.1,2,3)

(iv) Gautamasya Parkaḥ; Kaśyapasya Barhiṣyam; Gautamasyaiva Parkaḥ (GGG 1, 2, 3)

(v) Puruṣavratāni Pañca (AG. 132.1-)

(vi) Rauravam (Ūha.Daśa. 2)

(vii) Gautamasya Parkaḥ (GGG 1) [as per Anakavur tradition]

(II) Chanted by Pt. Dharmajña Rāmanātha Dīkṣita and his son Paṭṭābhirāma of Madras

(i) Bahiṣpavamānam (U.Ārc. Sūkta 1)

(ii) Ātrasāman (GGG. 284.2)

(iii) Gautamasya Parkaḥ (GGG 1)

(iv) Bhakāra Rathantaram (RG. 1)

(v) Yajñāyajñīyam (Ūha. Daśa. 14, First stotriyā)

(III) Chanted by Pt. Nārāyaṇa Aiyaṅgāra of Kumbhakonam and Pt. Jayarāmaśāstrī of Kunnur (recorded from the tape of Prof. E.R. Srikrishnasarma, at Tirupati)

(i) Āgneyakāṇḍa : Prathama Khaṇḍa (GGG 11-19)

(ii) Yajñāyajñīyasaman (GGG 35.4)

(iii) Pāvamānam (GGG 579 to 584.5)

(a) The four Aiṣirasāmans (GGG 579.1 to 4)

(b) The three Kārṇaśravasasāmans (GGG 580.1 to 3)

(c) The three Vācaḥsāmans (GGG 580.4 to 6)

(d) The two Kaulmalabarhiṣasāmans (GGG 581.1, 2)

(e) The Sādantīya-(Śaṅku)-sāman (GGG 581.3)

(f) The three Kaulmalabarhiṣasāmans (GGG 581.4 to 6)

(g) The two Loma-(Dīrgha)-sāmans (GGG 582.1, 2)

(h) The three Somasāmans (GGG 582. 3 to 5)

(i) The four Śaitoṣṇasāmans (GGG 583.1 to 4)

(j) The Gāyatrapārśvasāman (GGG 584.1)

(k) The Santanisāmaṇ (GGG 584.2)

(l) The three Somasāmans (GGG 584.3 to 5)

(IV) Chanted by Pt. Subrahmaṇyam Srauti of Mysore

(i) The Gāyatrasaman (at the beginning of GGG)

(ii) The three *Sāmans* : Gautamasya Parkah), Kaśyapasya Barhiṣyam and Gautamasyaiva Parkaḥ (GGG 1 to 3)

(iii) The Sāṁvargasāman (GGG 11.1)

(iv) The Rathantarasāman (Ūhya. 1.1.1)

(v) The Bṛhatsāman (AG. 14.1)

(vi) The Bārhaspatyasāman (GGG 91.1)

(vii) The Ājyadohasaman (AG. 25.1)

(viii) The Rauravasāman (Ūha. Daśa. 2)

(ix) The Yajñāyajñīyasāman (Ūha. Daśa. 14)

(x) Āmahīyavasāman (Ūha. Daśa. 1)

(V) (1) Kauthuma-Prācīna-style of Tanjore—(Putukode-style) (Recording sent by Shri L.S. Rajagopalan)

(a) Chanted by Pt. Gopāla Vādhyār

(i) Gāyatram (beginning of GGG)

(ii) Gautamasya Parkaḥ; Kasyapasya Barhiṣyam; Gautamasyāiva Parkaḥ (GGG 1-3)

(iii) The Bṛhatsāman (AG. 14.1)

(iv) The Rathantarasāman (AG. 49.1)

(v) The Rākṣoghnasāman (GGG 24. 1; 25.1)

(vi) The Mānavādyasāmans (GGG 54.1, 2)

(vii) The Hārivarṇasāmans (GGG 383. 1 to 4)

(viii) The Śukrasāman (AG. 89.1)

(b) Chanted by Śrī M.V. Nārāyaṇa Vādhyār of Manjupuram

(i) Gautamasya Parkaḥ; Kaśyapasya Barhiṣyam; Gautamasyaiva Parkaḥ (GGG 1, 2, 3)

(ii) The Āmahīyavasāman (Ūha. 1)

(iii) The Rathantarasāman (RG. Daśa. 1) (All the three stotrīyas)

(iv) The Vāmadevyasāman (Uha. Daśa. 5)

(v) The Bṛhatsāman (AG. 14.1)

(c) Chanted by Śrī Parameśvara Aiyar of Trikut village

(i) The Vāmadevyasāman (Ūha. Daśa. 5)

(ii) The Śrāyantīyasāman (GGG 267.1)

(2) Kauthuma Prācīna style of Anakavur chanted by Pt. Ekāmbaraśāstrī of Madras

(i) The Yajñāyajñīyasāman (Ūha. Daśa. 14)

(ii) The Mahāvaiśvāmitrasāman (Ūha. Daśa. 98; GGG. 343.6)

(iii) Gautamasya Parkaḥ (GGG 1)

(iv) The Rathantarasāman (AG. 49.1)

(v) The Kāvasāman (GGG 554.1)

(vi) Kaśyapasya Barhiṣyam (GGG 1.2)

(vii) The Śrāyantiyasāman (GGG 267.1)

Kauthuma (North) Gujarat style - chanted by Pt. Ṛṣiśaṅkara Tripāṭhī (Recorded from the tape of Vaidika Samshodhana Maṇḍaḷa, Pune)

(I) (i) The Bahiṣpavamānastotra (with Pañcadaśa stoma (Ūha. Ārc. Sūkta 1)

(ii) Ājyastotrāṇi—(Rathantarapṛṣṭha)

(1) First Ājyastotra (Ū. Ārc. Sūkta. 4)

The Gāyatrasāman.

(2) Second Ājyastotra (Ūha. P. 3 Sūkta. 5)

ā no mitrā. . .

(3) Third Ājyastotra (Ūha. P. 3) *ā y ā hi. . .*

(Sukta 6)

(4) Fourth Ājyastotra (Ūha. P. 4 Sūkta 7)

indrāgī āgatam. . .

(iii) Mādhyandinapavamāna

(1) Bhakāra Rathantara (Ūhya. 1)

(2) The Vāmadevyasāman (Ūha. Daśa. 5)

(3) The Naudhasasāman (Ūha. Daśa. 6)

(4) The Kāleyasāman(Ūha. Daśa. 7)

(5) The Rathantarasāman (with Saptadaśastoma).

(RG. Daśa. 1)

(II) Chanted by Pt. Mahādevaśarmāśāstrī of Surat (Gujarat)

(1) Setusaman (AG. 57.1)

(B) Rāṇāyanīya

(I) Havik Rāṇāyanīya of Karwar

(Chanted by Pt. Viśveśvara Rāmabhaṭṭa of Hosakole)

(i) Gautamasya Parkaḥ; Kaśyapasya Barhiṣyam; Gautamasyaiva Parkaḥ (GGG 1, 2, 3)

(a) (i) Bahiṣpavamānastotra (Ūha. Ārc. Sūkta 1 etc.)

(ii) The four Ājyastutis

(1) The First *stuti* - Gāyatram (U Ārc. Sūkta 4)

agna āyāhi . . .; and *agnim dūtam* . . .

(UĀrc. Sūkta 51)

(2) The second *stuti* (UĀrc. Sūkta. 5)

ā no mitrā . . .

(3) The third *stuti* (UĀrc. Sūkta 6)

ā yāhi. . .

(4) The fourth *stuti* (UĀrc. Sūkta 7)

indrāgnī ā...

(All these four belong to the Rathantarapṛṣṭha)

(b) The Mādhyandinapavamānastotra

Rathantarapṛṣṭha

(1) The Gāyatrasāman with *Okāras* (beginning with *hum)*

Ūha. Daśa. I - *uccā te* . . .

(2) The Rauravasāman (Ūha. Daśa. 2) Punānassoma . . .

(3) The Yaudhājayasāman (Ūha. Daśa. 3) *pu*^{3}*nā*^{2}

531

(4) Bhakārarathantaram (RG. 1.1)

(prathama pṛṣṭhastotra)

(5) Vāmadevyam - *ka ऽ5 yā . . .*

(dvitīya pṛṣṭhastotra (Ūha. Daśa. 5)

(6) Naudhasam (Ūha. Daśa. 6) *tā ऽ234mVO* (superscripts: 1 over tā, ra over VO)

(tṛtīya pṛṣṭhastotra)

(7) Kāleyam (Ūha. Daśa. 7)—*tarobhā 3. . .* (superscripts: 5ra over taro, 2 over bhā)

(caturtha pṛṣṭhastotra).

(c) Ārbhavapavamānastotra - Rathantarapṛṣṭha

(1) Gāyatram (UĀrc. Sūkta, 15)

hum/svādiṣṭhayā madiṣṭhayā//

(2) Saṁhitam (Ūha. Daśa. 8)

(3) Sapham (Ūha. Daśa. 9)

(4) Pauṣkalam (Ūha. Daśa. 10)

(5) Śyāvāśvam (Ūha. Daśa. 11)

(6) Āndhīgavam (Ūha. Daśa. 12)

(7) Kāvam (Ūha. Daśa. 13)

(i) Ārūḍhavadāṅgirasam (GGG 92.1)

(ii) Śyaitam (Ūha. Daśa. 43)

abhipravassurā/ . . .

(II) Rāṇāyanīya - Gurjarapāṭha—chanted by Pt. Avadhani and his companion of Siṁhācalam in Āndhra Pradesh. (GG. Agneyakāṇḍa - 1st khaṇḍa 1 to 19)

(III) Rāṇayanīya - Tāmraparṇipāṭha - chanted by Pt. Gopālaśāstrī and Pt. Nārāyaṇaśāstrī of Sitanagaram in Andhra (GGG Sāmans 1 to 30)

(IV) Chanted by Pt. Lakṣmaṇaśāstrī Dravid of Pune (originally his grandfather hailed from a village in the Tinnevelli District of South). (Recorded from the records in the Deccan College, Pune)

(i) Gāyatram (beginning of GGG)

(ii) The three Vyāhṛtisāmans (RG. Ahīna. 100)

(iii) The Jyeṣṭhasāma Ājyadoham (AG. 25.1)

(iv) Ādityasya Ātman (AG. 290)

(v) The first Tārkṣyasāman (GGG 332.1)

(vi) The Bṛhatsāman (Ūhya. Daśa. 5)

(C) Jaiminīya School

(a) Tamilnadu Jaiminīya

(Chanted by Pt. Rājagopāla Aiyaṅgāra and his pupils at Jaiminīya Pāṭhaśālā Śrīraṅgam)

(i) Gautamasya Parkaḥ; Kaśyapasya;

Barhiṣyam; Gautamasyaiva Parkaḥ.

(ii) Yajñāyajñīyam (Ūha. Daśa. 14)

(iii) Rathantaram (RG. 1.1) (1st stotriyā)

(iv) Ṛtusāman (GGG 321.1, 2)

(v) Ātrasāman (GGG 284.1.2)

(vi) Yaśassāman (AG. 61.1)

(vii) Rathantaravarṇam.

(b) Koḍuntarapuḷli Jaiminīya - (Chanted by Pt. Sahasranāma Aiyyar; Pt. Śrīnivāsa Aiyyar and three other Paṇḍits).

(i) Gautamasya Parkaḥ; Kaśyapasya Barhiṣyam; Gautamasyaiva Parkaḥ (GGG 1 to 3)

(ii) Ṛtusāman (RG. 321.1,2)

(iii) Rathantaram (RG. 1.1)

(iv) Gāyatram (Beginning of GGG)

(v) The fifth (Ilāndasāman (AG.126.1)

(vi) Angirasām Vratam (AG. 102.1)

(c) Nambudiri Jaiminīya—(Chanted by Pt. Tottam Subrahmaṇyam Nambudiripāda of Tottanilmana)

(i) Gautamasya Parkaḥ; Kaśyapasya Barhiṣyam; Gautamasyaiva Parkaḥ (GG. 1-3). Gautamasya

Parkaḥ is given below with the modern notation along with *kampa* as rendered by Miss Shirgopikar -

ओ ग्ना इ। आ या हि वा इ। ता

साऽरे निंरेसा सारेनिरेसा (4 times) सा सारेन्ंरेसा (thrice)

सारे निंरेसा सासा सारे न्ंरेसारे

या इ। ता या इ। गृ णा नो ह

न्ंरेसारे न्ंरेसा सा सारेन्ंरेसा सा न्ं सारेन्ंरेसा सारेसा रेसा

व्या दा। ता या इ

धंसारेन्ंरे सा न्ंरेसा सा सारेन्ंरेसा रे निरेसा सा।

ता या इ

सा सारे न्ंरेसा रेन्ंरेसा सा । ना इ हो ता

सारेन्ंरेसा रेन्ंरेसासा न्ंरेसारे न्ंरेसारे

सा । त्सा इ बा ।

न्ंरेसा (thrice) सा (thrice) सान्ंरेसा (twice) सा रेसरेन्ंरेसा (four times)

औ हो वा । ही[३] ऽ२ ३ ४ षी[५]

न्ं रेसा सान्ंरेसा (thrice) सा न्ंरेन्ंरे सारे न्ंरेसा सारे

न्ंरेसा (thrice) ।।

('हीषी' is stated here as per Kauthuma text.)

(ii) Ātrasāman (GGG. 284.2)

(iii) Pāvamānam (GGG. 511-9 to 16)

(iv) Pāvamānam (GGG. 512.1 to 15)

(v) *Asāvi soma* etc. (UĀrc. Sūkta. 128) (verses 378 to 380) three *Sāmans.*

(vi) Gāyatram (at the beginning of G.G.G.)

(vii) Jamadagneḥ Arkaḥ (AG. 15.2)

(viii) Ūṣāṇi (1) Rathantaram;

(ix) Vāravantīyam (GGG Sūkta 288, UĀrc. 920, 921, 922)

Andhra tradition of Guntur Region (Chanted by Pt. Prof. Laxminarayana of Hyderabad)

(i) Pravadbhārgavam (GGG 557-3)

(ii) Śyaitam (GGG. 235.3)

(iii) Ūhyagāna (UArc. Sūkta. 386)

(iv) Śukrasāman (AG. 89.1)

(v) Payassāman (AG. 70.1)

(D) Bhāruṇḍasāman (At the end of AG.)

(Recording made available to me by Prof. J.F. Staal from his recordings.)

(There is no underlying *ṛc*. It consists largely of stobhas. The chanter is from Saurashtra). This sāman is said to resemble the song of a particular bird.

Glossary

Atikrama — Descent to lower note dropping one or more intermediate notes; e.g. ū^{11}ʃ2 (GGG. 284.2)

Atihāra — Anusvāra, Sparśa and Repha, when followed by stobha, are joined to the syllable of the *ṛc*, crossing over the stobha e.g. tsā^{1}ʃ2ibā^{3}ʃ234 au$^{5ra\ ra}$hovā । hī^{3}ʃ234ʃī^{5} ॥ (G.G.G.1.1); there is pause at the end of the *stobha* hence the consonant *r* is elided. When there is Sandhi, the elision is not there e.g. vā^{1ra}jā^{3ra}nā^{2}ūsau । vāʃ343^{2}0ʃ34vā^{5} । pa^{4}tā . . .। (the consonant *t* is elided [Ūha Prā 802] (sātpati); in the *saṁhitā t* is not elided in the case of *satpatim.* Anusvāra and sparśa should be followed by the syllable of its own class and the Repha in conjunction with the sparśa and Ūṣman, in regard to Atihāra ..ʃ vauh$^{[5]ra}$o̲r̲ṇā^{5}rām (*svarṇaram*) [*r* is joined to *ṇaram* crossing the *stobha auho*. GGG.109.3]

Adhyardheḍā	The Nidhana of the nature of *it iḍā.*
Adhyāsyā	In it the fourth quarter of the second *ṛc* of the *tṛca* is repeated and Dvipadāvirāj is employed; thus the number of syllables required for the Bṛhatī metre is achieved (8+8+12+8 = 36 syllables) [UArc *Sūkta* 198, Ūha. Sam 267]
Antaḥsāmika	The Nidhana used in the midst of the *Sāman.*
Antarṇidhana	The Nidhana formed by the wording of the *ṛc.*
Anvayikī	Fully agreeable with each quarter.
Anvayin	The *stobha* at the beginning of a word.
Anuṣaṅgin	The *stobha* that follows a word.
Anudātta	Grave accent.
Āvirgāna	Chanting of the *ṛc* only without *stobha.*
Udātta	Acute accent.
Upagāna	In it the co-chanters employ the syllable *ho* sung in Mandra note, continually till the Nidhana.
Upagraha	The vowel *e* chanted preceding the Nidhana.
Upāya	The Nidhana *vā.*
Karṣaṇa	Pulling of the note downwards.
Gāthā	The *ṛc* praising the deity, e.g. Yamagāthā

Channagāna	The chanting of the *Sāman* based on the *stobhas* only (the chant thus has concealed nature).
Channani-dhana	The Nidhana, concealed in another form at the time of daily practice, is revealed in its real form when the *Sāman* is employed in rituals.
Tṛcagāna	Chanting with the three *ṛcs* of the *sūkta.*
Triṣṭubh	The Vedic metre of four quarters having eleven syllables in each quarter.
Padastobha	The *stobha* in the form of a word; e.g. *atha, iha*, etc.
Padanidhana	The Nidhana formed by the word of the *ṛc.*
Padānusvāra	It has the form ^{5}656. It is marked by nasalization. It is called Parisvāra also.
Pracaya	The Anudātta syllables coming after the *svarita* (circumflex accent) are called Pracaya. They are left unmarked like Udātta.
Parisāman	The *Sāman* which only the Prastotṛ chants.
Pṛṣṭha	There are two *pṛṣṭas* namely, Rathantara and Bṛhat. The *Sāmans* are stated under each *pṛṣtha.*
Puṣpa	According to some, it is the name of the sage who composed Puṣpasūtra; according to Dr.

	Sharma it means the syllabic modification effected in regard to *Sāman*.
Bahirṇidhana	The Nidhana formed by the syllables outside those of the *ṛc*.
Bhakti	The division of the *Sāman*. The Bhaktis are five, namely Prastāva, Udgītha, Pratihāra, Upadrava and Nidhana. By the addition of Om two times, the divisions become seven.
Mātrā	Unit of time-measure which is equal to the duration of utterance of one short syllable.
Mīṇḍa	A fast-moving descent with smooth gliding.
Yajus	The prose formula employed in the sacrifice.
Yoni	(1) the *ṛc* on which the *Sāman* is based; (2) the first *ṛc* of the *tṛca*, the *Sāman* based on which is employed in the other two *ṛcs* of the *tṛca*.
Roha	Ascent.
Rūpāntara	The form of *Sāman* used in one's own daily recital.
Vṛtti	The mode of chanting such as slow, medium or fast.

Vinarda — The chanting of the particular note resembling the sound of a bull.

Visvara — The note which due to pulling downwards attains the position of another note, e.g. $\overset{1}{0}$ʃ2345i - in this illustration the vowel *o* having *prathamasvara* is pulled down to the *mandrasvara*.

Vṛdhesvara — The last syllable of the *ṛc* having Udātta accent becomes Vṛdhesvara in the chant e.g. śriy$\overset{2}{e}$ʃ1

Veyagāna — Prakṛtigāna or Pūrvagāna.

Stobha — The syllables in addition to the syllables of the *ṛc* like *hāu*, *vā* etc. It is of three types - Varṇastobha (the *stobha* in the form of syllable), Padastobha (the *stobha* in the form of a word) and Vākyastobha the *stobha* in the form of a sentence or phrase).

Stotrīyā — The *Sāman* with five divisions forms the *stotrīyā*.

Svārya — The last syllable of the *ṛc* or *stobha* having Svarita accent becomes *svārya* in the chant e.g. $\overset{2}{s}$uvirvid$\overset{3}{ā}$ ^{111}ʃ2345ḥ.

Bibliography

Akṣaratantra, edited by M. Rāmānātha Dīkṣita, Madras, 1934. (Stobhabhāṣyam-Akṣaratantram, pp. 99-162)

Ārṣeyakalpa of Maśaka, with the Commentary of Varadarāja, ed. by Dr. B.R. Sharma, Hoshiyarpur, 1976.

Das Puspasūtra mit Einleitung und Ubersetzung by Richard Simon, Munich, 1908.

Grāmegeyagānam-Āraṇyakagānam, edited by Nārāyaṇasvāmi Dīkṣita, Svādhyāya Maṇḍal, Aundh, 1942.

Mātrālakṣaṇam by Dr. Wayne Howard, New Delhi, 1988.

Lāṭyāyanaśrautasūtra, published by Munshiram Manoharlal Publishers, Pvt. Ltd., 2nd edition, New Delhi, 1982.

Nāradīyaśikṣā, Shripitambarapitha Sanskrit Pariṣad, Datia, 1964.

Pratihārasūtra, edited by Dr. B.R. Sharma, Kendrīya Sanskrit Vidyapeetha, Tirupati, 1973.

Sāmavedic Chant by Wayne Howard, New Haven and London, Yale University Press, 1977.

Sāmagāna Kriyā Paddhati (Hindi) by Pandit Mahādevasharma Śāstri, Pandit Mahādevasharma Śāstri Grantha Prakashan Samiti, Surat, 1984.

Sāmatantra, edited by Pandit Rāmanātha Dīkṣita, Banaras Hindu University, Varanasi, 1961.

Sāmavedīya-Rudrajapavidhi, editor, Pandit Ṛṣiśaṅkara Agnihotri, Varanasi, 1963.

Saṁhitopaniṣad Brāhmaṇa, edited by Dr. B.R. Sharma, Devatādhyaya-Saṁhitopaniṣad-Vamśa-Brāhmaṇas, Kendrīya Sanskrit Vidyapeetha, Tirupati, 1965.

Sāmavidhānabrāhmaṇa, edited by B.R. Sharma, Kendrīya Sanskrit Vidyapeetha Series No. 1, Tirupati, 1964.

Studies on the Sāmaveda, Part I by Barend Faddegon, Amsterdam, North Holland Publishing Company, 1951.

Svarapakriyāprakāśa (Hindi) by Dr. Vāmadevamiśra, Varanasi, 1975.

Tāṇḍyabrāhmaṇa, Chaukhamba Sanskrit Series, Banaras, Vol. I, 1935 and Vol. II, 1936.

The Four Vedas, by Prof. J.F. Staal, Asch Mankind Series, New York, 1968.

The Literature and Study of the Jaiminīya Sāmaveda - In Retrospect and Prospect by Asko Parpola, Helsinki, 1973.

The Puṣpasūtram, edited by M. Rāmanātha Dikṣitār, Madras, 1989.

The Ṣaḍviṁśabrāhmaṇa, The Ārṣeyabrāhmaṇa, the Jaiminīya Upaniṣadbrāhmaṇas, edited by Dr. B.R. Sharma, Kendrīya Sanskrit Vidyapeetha, Tirupati, 1967.

The Vedic Chant Studied in its Textual and Melodic Form, by J.M. Van der Hoogt, Wageningen, 1929.

Ūhagānam-Ūhyagānam, edited by A.M. Rāmanātha Dīkṣita, Banaras Hindu University, Varanasi, 1967.

Vaidika Paramparāme Sāmagāna (Hindi), Translation of Rajyeshwar Mitra's Bengali work by Madanlal Vyas, Varanasi, 1978.

Vaidika Saṅgīta (Marathi) by Dhundirajashastri Bapat, Poona, Bharat Gayan Samaj, Pune, 1954.

Vaidika-Svara-Mīmāṁsā by Yudhiṣṭhira Mīmāmsaka, Varanasi, 1936.

Veyagāna-Araṇyagāna, V.T. Rajan Press, Madras, 1967.

The Prapāṭhakas 1 & 2 of the Puṣpasūtra with the Commentary of Nānābhāi Dīkṣita, Manuscript.

Some Reflections on the Notations of Vedic Chant, by Walter Kaufmann, Bloomington, 1968, pp. 1-18.

The Journal of the Indian Musicological Society, Baroda, Vol. XX, Nos. 1 & 2, June and December, 1989, pp. 5 to 16.

Studies in the Accentuation of the Sāmaveda by Dr. Siddheshwar Varma, All India Oriental Conference (1930); Vol. VI, B.O.R.I., Poona.

'The Concept of Key-note in the Taittirīya Prātisākhya' by C.R. Sankaran; Journal of Oriental Research, Madras, Vol. 14 and Vol. 15.

The Cassette having the recording of the Shomyo of Japan sent to me by my student Nobuyoshi ASAI of Japan.